THE INDUSTRIAL REVOLUTION EXPLAINED

Steam, Sparks and Massive Wheels

STAN YORKE

COUNTRYSIDE BOOKS
NEWBURY BERKSHIRE

First published 2005
© Stan Yorke 2005

COUNTRYSIDE BOOKS
3 Catherine Road
Newbury, Berkshire

To view our complete range of books,
please visit us at
www.countrysidebooks.co.uk

ISBN 1 85306 935 3
EAN 978185306 935 2

Photographs by the author
Line illustrations by Trevor Yorke

Produced through MRM Associates Ltd., Reading
Typeset by Techniset Typesetters, Newton-le-Willows
Printed by Woolnough Bookbinding Ltd., Irthlingborough

CONTENTS

Introduction

The words 'industry' and 'revolution' are strange bedfellows. The first might well conjure up huge pistons, spinning wheels and hissing steam but to most people these days it is, alas, a rather vague term. The second probably brings images of war and sadness based on the oft-told stories of the French Revolution. So what happened here in England that earned itself this strange label?

Generally taken as the period from 1750 to 1850, the Industrial Revolution was, in fact, the application of better manufacturing methods and new sources of power and materials to long-established products. This simple description is, however, far too mild; the changes were truly amazing and affected every walk of life. Someone from the 12th or 13th centuries could have wandered around England in 1700 and would not have felt lost. They

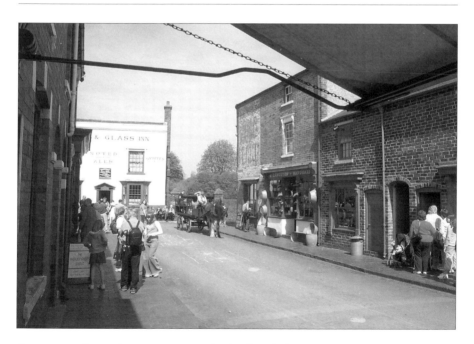

A summer's day in late Victorian England. The Black Country Living Museum.

The reception and entrance to the North of England Open Air Museum, Beamish.

would have been impressed with the improved river navigations, better housing and greater academic knowledge, but little else. But taking someone from 1700 and putting them down in, say, 1850 would have been like space travel!

Interest in this unique 100-year period has slowly reawakened in recent years, often spurred on by TV documentaries. There are now over 500 museums related to industry in the British Isles, from small sites open just a few days a month to superb modern displays using all the latest visual techniques to tell their stories. Many original machines and processes survive from the Victorian period, plus many examples of processes that have

changed little since the 16th century. Where the story becomes slightly misty is how this vast industrial world started, but enquire how the machines and processes actually work and you will find the mist has turned to darkest fog! It is not that we don't know, it is simply that the detail is buried in lofty volumes that can make rather heavy reading. This book tries to bridge the gap by explaining some of the background and workings of the machines without getting too complex.

Today, so extensive is our knowledge that we can make almost anything. Driven by a world of marketing, we expect a continuous flow of new products, each better than or different from its predecessor. In reality, though, very few are really new; instead they are simply the result of applying new manufacturing techniques and materials to old ideas. It is slightly unnerving, when looking back at our industrial history, to find just how many basic ideas belong to a time that is not just a decade or two ago but several centuries earlier.

In the first section of the book, I sketch in the historical background to the revolution to show that this was a steady accumulation of knowledge and skills and not at all a sudden step change. In Section II I look in detail at four major industrial areas that are well represented in our museums and see how the basic machines work and how the processes were developed.

Section III examines some of the other areas involved in supporting the vast expansion, not necessarily in the direct line of the revolution, but vitally interwoven into it.

Finally, Section IV gives some ideas for finding more information, and lists some of the larger multi-subject museums – along with some surprising statistics.

If your image of an industrial museum is dark, dusty and boring, then prepare to be pleasantly surprised. Hopefully, this little book will contribute to your enjoyment.

Stan Yorke

Cast iron bridge and pump house resting at peace with the world, just outside Coventry. A classic example of items from the Industrial Revolution now surrounded by modern-day housing.

The winding house for the Middleton Incline on the Cromford and High Peak railway. Though the line is long gone, the steam engine inside is still working.

SECTION I

A
BRIEF
HISTORY

CHAPTER I

Setting the Scene

✦

The history of industry is a fascinating world of interdependent discoveries and processes, which developed almost independently from – indeed, one could say, despite – the more familiar world of kings and queens and politics.

To most of us the word 'industry' conjures up factories producing cars, processed foods, furniture and so on. Add the word 'heritage' and our eyes turn misty with romantic thoughts of the Victorian era, ornate brass-covered pumps and engines, dark satanic mills and mines. But to find the roots of the Industrial Revolution we must look much further back than the Victorians, indeed practically all the real inventing was over by the start of that worthy reign.

We know that the Egyptians were spinning and weaving flax to produce linen at least 4,000 years ago. Glass making is known to date from a similar period. By 100 BC the waterwheel had been devised and mechanised grinding of flour started. So good was the Romans' grasp of technology that by the 3rd century at Barbell, near Arles, in southern France they had constructed a flight of eight pairs of waterwheels spaced down a 65 ft slope. The water came from a reservoir, which, in turn, was fed by aqueducts in typical Roman fashion. The sixteen grind wheels produced enormous quantities of flour – enough for 80,000 people. Thought to be the largest 'industrial' complex in the Roman Empire, it was made special by its supply chain. Grain was brought to Arles not just from the surrounding area but by ship from as far away as Egypt. The flour was then sent north hundreds of miles to feed the Roman armies of occupation. This was, in fact, the basic factory operation that we are all familiar with today.

Here in England, once the Romans had left, we went through a period of enormous turmoil. Wars, invasions and plagues instilled a rare mix of character that possibly made us more able to accept change than many other European nations. Despite the overlay of kings and their armies raging around, ordinary life continued, as did the spread of the technology of the day. A hint of this comes from the Domesday Book written around 1085 where over 6,000 waterwheels are recorded, most employed in grinding corn for flour.

The main activity after agriculture involved wool, and this was centred on Wiltshire with smaller areas in East Anglia and Yorkshire. English wool was much sought after and we exported almost all we could produce, creating very rich families who left their mark in the form of some beautiful churches. So valued was English wool that it constituted the ransom for the return of Richard the Lionheart.

Weaving and cloth production were carried out in the home using a vertical loom, a slow and labour-intensive process. The horizontal loom arrived, like many ideas at this time, from the Continent, sometime in the 1300s, as did the windmill, which joined the waterwheel as a second source of power.

By the dawn of the 15th century we can see the slow start of new thinking and invention, though still governed by religious dogma and the belief in the ideas of Aristotle, both of which discouraged practical experiments.

Clocks had also arrived from the Continent, used solely to regulate ecclesiastical rituals, there being as yet no need for time-keeping as we think of it. These devices, however, introduced the idea of mechanisms using gears and springs, and by the 1500s had developed into watches and clocks that we would easily recognise today.

This spread of knowledge led to an increase in the demand for books throughout Europe, although they were still only produced by scribes, who copied by hand onto parchment. As the years went by, worn out linen, now widely available, was collected to make paper. Initially this was a job done by those who previously collected bones for fertiliser – hence, the rag and bone man.

Paper made this way was much cheaper than parchment, resulting in a less expensive book, but this just helped the demand for written works to grow and soon scribes couldn't keep up. It

FIG 1.1: *An early clock mechanism showing gears, pawls and ratchet. This type of mechanism would have driven a small outside clock, probably on a church. This example is on display in the Nottingham Industrial Museum.*

FIG 1.2: *Early printing press. The paper was held in a frame, which hinged down over the ready inked typeface. This sandwich was then inserted under the press, which simply held the two together in order to transfer the ink. This example is in the Leeds Industrial Museum, Armley Mills.*

was this shortage that drove the search for some form of automatic writing machine and by the late 1400s the problem was solved. Printing using movable typeface had been invented and, at a stroke, it transformed laborious hand copying into an industry that introduced a new concept – rapid distribution of news. Its effects were to be far reaching and way beyond the aspirations of those who sought to improve the hand copying process. Brought to these shores from Bruges by William Caxton in 1476, within four years there were printing works in four English towns.

All printing was still controlled by the Church until 1557 when Henry VIII formed the Stationers' Company. He limited the country to just 21 printers, all of them in London. This royal control lasted until 1695 though the regulations were frequently ignored before this. Not only were there now relatively cheap and accurate copies of works like the Bible (still in Latin) but for the first time it was possible to pass on technical information. Indeed 'How to do it' books on metallurgy, farming and machines were the next most common type of book after the Bible.

There is an interesting comment to be

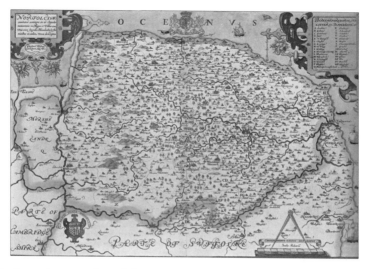

FIG 1.3: *Saxton's map of Norfolk. It shows 26 market towns and a staggering 625 villages. There is also the first attempt at showing relief. These maps were heavily biased towards featuring the lands owned by the rich, particularly those held in favour by Queen Elizabeth I.*

found here in the attitude to solving problems. The early printing presses and reusable type were developed to replace the scribe and his slow, often inaccurate hand copying. But the first presses just replicated what the scribes did. The typeface was a copy of a good hand script, and the larger decorative figures and the embellished first letter of a paragraph were simply left out of the printing process. This particular point is rather ironic since, for a long time before printing presses arrived, these features had been made by applying hand-cut wood blocks, wetted with coloured inks, and not by the scribe using pen and inks. But it took another 30 years before someone thought of improving the script-style typeface to produce a more easily readable form of print. This inability to see beyond the immediate problem characterises all the early developments and, as we shall see, this did not really change until the entrepreneur arrived on the scene in the 1750s.

The 16th and 17th centuries produced a flood of advances in thinking and knowledge. William Tyndale translated the Bible into English, which probably helped standardise our language more than any other event. Robert Recorde set out mathematics in a formal and understandable way and, in particular, he published it in book form. This is the time of Galileo and Shakespeare and some of our most momentous history.

At Queen Elizabeth's request,

FIG 1.4: *Typical horse-drawn coach – it doesn't take much imagination to understand that journeying in one of these for hours must have been quite an ordeal.*

Christopher Saxton produced the first accurate maps of England – not, I hasten to add, maps like those of the Ordnance Survey, but depictions that enabled travellers to grasp the overall layout of the country and the relative positions of towns and cities. He surveyed all 52 counties of England and Wales between 1574 and 1579 – a quite remarkable achievement.

The first dedicated clean water supply for London was a conduit that ran from near Ware, in Hertfordshire, and it still supplies water to this day.

Horse-drawn taxi services started in London and other large towns. Long-distance coach services started – though not quite what we think of today. To give an example, the service from London to Chester reached Coventry in two days, Stone on the third and Chester on the fourth. The experience was described as suitable only for the strong!

We had arrived at a time when men were questioning why things happened the way they did, pitting their own observations against the accepted doctrines. Many of these new ideas upset the Church, which tried in vain to suppress them.

CHAPTER 2

Science Replaces Dogma

To the average peasant, the understanding of new techniques or machines was totally alien; the rule was: 'We've always done it this way, so why change?' This is nicely illustrated by the story of Jethro Tull, the agriculturalist, who was born in 1674. He believed that the yield from seeds would be better if they were planted at precise gaps in widely spaced rows, rather than the traditional method of sowing as many seeds as possible, close together. His farm workers were so furious at the cheek of this pen pusher (Tull had trained in law) telling them their job that they promptly went on strike! So, provoked, Tull set about designing an automatic seed drill to do the job his way. Most farmers laughed but the improved yields soon spoke volumes and a revolution in farming had started.

Like Tyndale, Recorde and Saxton, Francis Bacon produced written works that had a far greater effect on the coming generations than he could have imagined. Between 1610 and 1620 Bacon suggested a fundamental change in the way science was practised. He challenged the age-old idea of Aristotle, that knowledge could be gained by wise men debating. Instead he proposed a culture of careful experiment, testing and measuring. His ideas attracted many like-minded men and eventually, with the king's interest aroused, he founded the Royal Society of London for Improving Natural Knowledge, which was to form the linchpin of the subsequent expansion of the pure sciences.

The circulation of human blood was explained – earlier ideas on this were frankly hilarious. Better optical instruments, involving grinding glass to a precise shape, enabled the microscope to be made, showing us creatures never seen before, like fleas. Telescopes and better mathematics solved the long-mysterious problems of the skies, and the old astronomical ideas were turned on their heads. The same optics produced early reading glasses, though concave lenses needed to correct short sightedness had to wait another century.

It is refreshing to discover just how many products and processes were invented way before the time we think of as the industrial periods of our history. By 1650 much of our basic technical knowledge existed. All our familiar organised activities such as defence, agriculture, metalwork, building and transportation were well established, albeit in a form which

FIG 2.1: *The Culpepper pattern compound microscope of around 1750. This was the first serious microscope to be produced in large quantities.*

Firstly, all the developments and inventions were made in direct response to a need. The great marketing powers that now convince us that we really need some product or other didn't exist. The inventor had the help of skilled craftsmen to design and construct his 'machine'. It was the knowledge of the craftsmen and the materials available that constrained the progress of the inventor, not the lack of problems to be solved. Also, once the perceived need had been met, no further exploration of the new devices was undertaken. Improvements did occur but mostly from local craftsmen who incorporated their own ideas as they copied the original invention for use in their own areas.

Secondly, almost everything was individually made; this meant that every item was slightly different from the next. If a cartwheel broke, the local wheelwright made a replacement to the dimensions of the broken one. Nobody had yet conceived the benefits of standardised parts.

It is very easy to get the impression that the industrial skills that developed through these 3,000 odd years were very basic and crude. Indeed, at the everyday village level they were, but a small percentage of craftsmen achieved standards that were exceptional. Invariably these men worked for the rich – the Church and the rulers. They produced spectacular results – from the pyramids and tombs of Egypt to the more familiar cathedrals and abbeys of England.

nowadays we would describe as cottage industries. One possible exception being naval dockyards which were already becoming embryo factories. Each individual factory or organisation would employ typically two or three people, with really large companies rarely employing more than ten. But every large village or town now had its own set of basic craftsmen.

Pure science had been formalised and recognised at the highest level; mathematics and science seemed on the brink of being able to understand almost anything. We must also note some aspects of this progress that seem slightly strange to us today.

Visit any large museum and you will find exquisite artefacts produced by the

FIG 2.2: *Though from a later date this chain-making workshop gives the feel of a large company of the 1700s. Avoncroft Museum of Historic Buildings.*

early metalworker, potter and carpenter. In general, none of these outstanding products used anything that was not widely available; it was simply that the wealthy could allow the top craftsman to have time and the best materials, luxuries that ordinary life could not afford.

By the start of the 18th century, industry had a vast range of materials plus much new knowledge, but a new breed of person was needed to apply these to everyday life. And sure enough the entrepreneur, the man with the far-sighted vision of what might be possible, duly appeared.

Though both of immense importance to industrial growth, just two fundamental developments remained to be made – the steam engine and better transport, the latter provided by canals at first and then railways. Oddly, neither arrived with a bang; both developed slowly and without any realisation of their potential.

Look around and consider what we see today – roads, public and private transport, shops, doctors, hospitals, schools, books and art. Add in houses, pubs, theatres, central heating, running water, washing machines, carpets, furniture, music and orchestras, artificial lighting. They all existed in 1700! True, much was in a simple form that we would think of as plain hard work.

What followed was a massive improvement of these products and this is partly why there was such speed in accepting the changes. People often comment on the extraordinary way mobile phones have become an everyday thing. The point is that we all knew what a phone was; the mobile phone was simply an improvement and thus was accepted readily. The same thing happened in the Industrial Revolution, as each aspect of our lives got better. The middle class evolved, enjoying cheaper food, clothes and housing. Transport enabled travel in a way never dreamt of before. Although the lot of the poor was probably as bad as ever, there was a massive sense of achievement and national pride.

So let's look at some of the most important areas of industry and see just how they changed and developed. I've chosen subjects that are well represented in our modern museums – with an unashamed bias towards things that go round!

FIG 2.3: *We are approaching the era when the horse would no longer be supreme. These horse gins were very common in mining before the arrival of steam engines. This replica is at the Magpie lead mine in the Peak District National Park, west of Bakewell.*

SECTION II

STARS

OF THE

SHOW

CHAPTER 3

Wheels from the Past

FIG 3.1: *The quintessential mill. This is Barnwell Mill on the river Nene in Cambridgeshire, now converted to a restaurant but once a busy flour mill with at least two breastshot waterwheels.*

You may well ask why I have chosen this subject at all since waterwheels existed long before the Industrial Revolution. The fact is that they were still our main source of power even at the beginning of the 18th century and without the waterwheel the revolution simply could not have happened.

The earliest waterwheels were the Norse wheels, which worked like a simple turbine. They turned a vertical shaft, so the grinding stones could be directly driven. There are, however, no examples left in England.

The normal type of waterwheel is

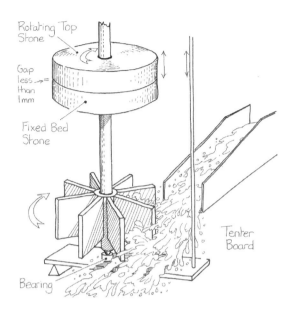

Rotating Top Stone

Gap less → = than 1mm

Fixed Bed Stone

Bearing

Tenter Board

FIG 3.2: *Diagrammatic view of the early Norse wheel. These were basic turbines, which were to reappear many centuries later in a much more sophisticated form. The grindstones would have been smaller than we are used to seeing today.*

FIG 3.3: *The basic Vitruvius undershot waterwheel. Though the path of the water can be constrained so that all the water must pass under the wheel, this is little more than a Norse wheel on its side. Its much larger diameter, however, allows the shaft to be kept well above the stream. Relatively easy to build and maintain.*

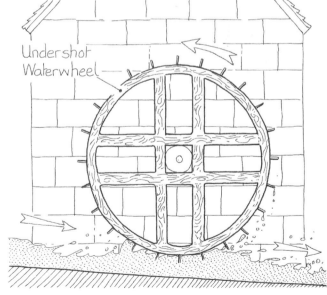

Undershot Waterwheel

known as a Vitruvius wheel, named after the Roman engineer who first described them. Their design involved a quite complex balance between diameter, width and the features of the river water they used. Rivers, unfortunately, do not flow steadily all year round, a problem that was partly solved by building a weir across the river to hold back a considerable length of water – the mill pond. From one end of this pond a channel would be created, which fed the waterwheel.

This simple idea brought two desirable features: it allowed great quantities of flood water to pass over the weir in winter without raising the mill pond water level too much, and the feed channel (leat or leete) allowed the water flow to the wheel to be controlled or indeed turned off completely.

The design of the wheel itself was governed by three factors: how far the water had to fall (determined by the weir height); how much water was available; and the strength of the

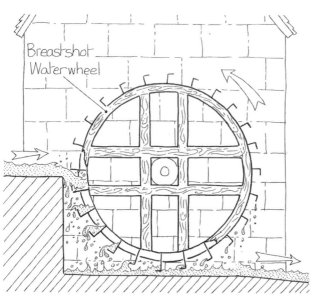

FIG 3.4: *Probably the most common arrangement – the breastshot wheel. This depends on either a weir or a long leat taken from well up the stream that feeds it. The power now comes partly from the weight of the water and partly from its speed.*

FIG 3.5: *A later improvement ran the stonework tight to the curve of the wheel, thus preventing any water from escaping before all its energy had been put into the wheel. Combined with a curved bucket these changes increased the efficiency from around 20% to well over 50%.*

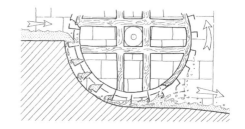

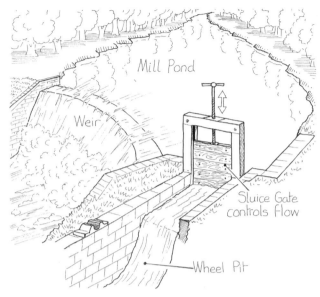

FIG 3.6: *This drawing shows the principal parts of a small rural mill pond. There are hundreds of ponds like this on streams around the country even though the mill may have long vanished.*

FIG 3.7: *Some mill ponds grew to enormous size like this spinning mill weir pond in Belper, Derbyshire, which extends above the weir for over ½ mile up the river Derwent.*

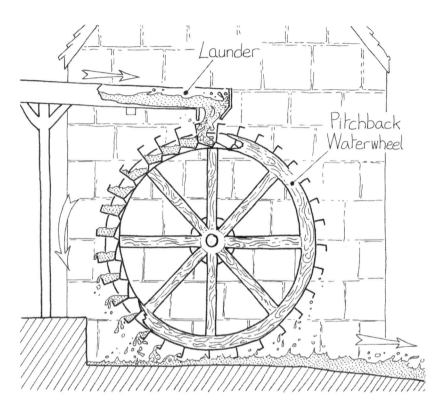

FIG 3.8: *The largest diameter wheels were the overshot and pitchback wheels. The overshot wheel lets the water flow naturally onto the wheel top but this turns the wheel in the opposite direction to breastshot or undershot wheels. Quite often these larger diameter wheels were installed to replace a smaller breastshot wheel. This meant all the machinery in the mill would have to change direction. A much cheaper option was to use the pitchback wheel as shown above. This loses a little of the energy but turns the wheel the same way as a breastshot wheel.*

materials, in particular, the main shaft that conveyed the rotating energy from the wheel into the mill. Early wheels tended to be two to three metres in diameter and no more than one metre wide. Most were undershot, where the speed of the water matters, or breastshot, where the weight of the water provides most of the energy. There was a basic limit on the torque that could be carried along the wooden shaft without it breaking and this limited the size of the early wheels. Where the water supply was plentiful, it was the usual practice to build more than one wheel within the same mill building, all fed from the same mill pond. Mills with three or four wheels were not uncommon.

Where the river or stream dropped steeply, it was possible to take the leat from greater heights and then tip the water onto the top of the wheel – the overshot wheel. This made maximum use of the weight of the water and allowed a narrower wheel to produce the same energy as a normal-sized breastshot wheel. It usually involved taking the water to the top of the wheel in some form of elevated channel (launder), originally constructed of wood.

One rather special mill was the tidal mill, which had the mill pond filled by the incoming tide and then ran the water back to sea via the waterwheel. Although limited to working in sympathy with the tides, it did have the virtue of not running out of water! As ironwork improved in the 1700s

FIG 3.9: *At Morwellham Quay in Devon you can see this large diameter overshot wheel, which used to power a manganese grinding mill.*

more and more of the wooden parts were replaced. First joints would be strengthened, particularly around the main shaft, and later the shaft itself would be cast in iron along with the main bearings. The spokes, launders and eventually the whole wheel were produced in iron by the 1800s.

Though we tend to think of the waterwheel producing a rotating motion, some were built to drive pumps using a crank to give a to and fro motion. Often the waterwheel was located a long way from the mines or pits that were being pumped out, and the to and fro motion was transmitted by long runs of stout wooden or iron beams running on rollers between the waterwheel and the pumps. The greatest of these is on the Isle of Man, at Laxey. Built in 1854, with a 72 ft 6 in (22 m) diameter wheel, the pump beams travelled 450 yards (412 m) to the pumps.

FIG 3.10: *This breastshot wheel shows the mix of wood and iron. The shaft is a casting along with the rim but the spokes and paddles are still wood. This mill at Cheddleton near Stoke on Trent is another water-driven mill that was converted from flour grinding to serve early industry. It ground flint for use in the nearby pottery industries.*

FIG 3.11: *This 35 ft (10 m) diameter pitchback wheel turned a crank (right) which drove rods used to pump china clay slurry from the nearby pits at the Wheal Martyn China Clay Museum in Cornwall.*

The waterwheel itself would turn far too slowly for the grindstones used in milling so it was normal for the drive to be taken to the grindstones via at least two step-up gears. Made of wood until cast iron took over in the late 1700s, the first gears (pit wheel and wallower) would turn the drive from a horizontal to vertical direction and increase the speed by around three times. This vertical shaft carried the large spur gear which, in turn, drove typically two smaller gears (stone nut) that turned the grinding stones.

Most grinding stones rotated around 150 to 250 times a minute which would seem pretty frightening for anyone standing close by. Right to the end of waterwheel construction, wooden teeth (beech, apple wood or pear wood) were often used for one of the gears to prevent having a metal to metal contact which could produce a spark – the risk of igniting the flour dust was very real. These wooden teeth also kept the noise made by the gears to a low level and, in the event of a major jamming, they would shear off rather than ruin the cast wheels and the shafts.

The need to turn the stones much faster than the wheel rotated was later met by taking the power from the rim of the waterwheel rather than the centre shaft. A strong cast iron gear track

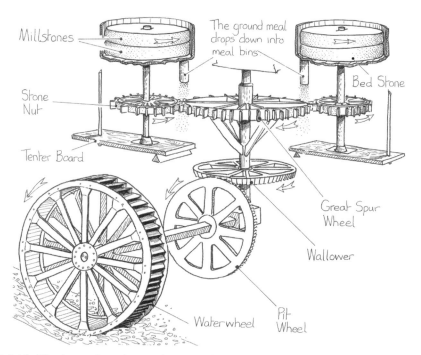

Millstones

The ground meal drops down into meal bins

Bed Stone

Stone Nut

Tenter Board

Great Spur Wheel

Wallower

Waterwheel

Pit Wheel

FIG 3.12: *The internal workings of a typical waterwheel-driven flour mill. The gearing not only changes the horizontal drive from the wheel to vertical but provides the increase in speed needed for the stones. The tenter board allows the entire top stone and its shaft to be raised or lowered to adjust the gap between the grinding stones. The lower bed stone is always fixed in position and stationary.*

would be fitted around the outer edge of the wheel, which drove a smaller gear wheel mounted on a shaft that entered the mill. This rotated much faster than the waterwheel itself and reduced the need to have massive gearing inside the mill.

This development had another, not so obvious, benefit. When the drive was taken from the centre shaft of a waterwheel, the power had to be taken from the circumference, where the water was falling, and be transmitted to the centre shaft via the spokes. Thus, the spokes were not just holding the wheel in shape but were also carrying the turning forces. This evoked a need for considerable strength not only in the spokes themselves but also in their joints, which were subject to an enormous twisting action. By taking the drive from the circumference, the spokes were now only carrying the weight of the wheel and not the torque. The spokes were just in tension and the joints did not

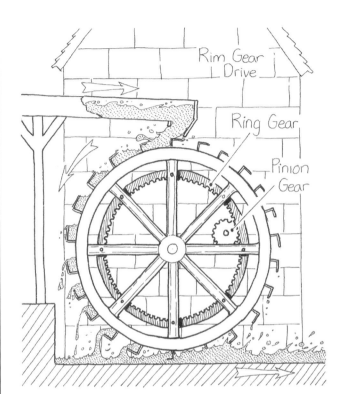

FIG 3.13: *A rim gear drive on a pitchback wheel. This form of drive was used for many applications as well as flour grinding.*

FIG 3.14: *The real thing at Daniels Mill near Bewdley in Shropshire. This flour mill originally used a breastshot wheel but later changed to this pitchback wheel. This, in turn, is now operated as a breastshot wheel. Changes like this were very common over the centuries.*

experience any twisting action. The centre shaft was also relieved of transmitting the torque. This allowed the construction of the spokes and centre shaft to be much lighter (and cheaper) than a conventional centre-driven wheel.

The virtue of the waterwheel was its relative cheapness and virtually zero running costs. These factors kept waterwheel construction going up to the 1850s, with units able to produce up to 200 horse power. The only problem was that they depended on the stream or river not running dry. Processes like grinding corn could be held back for a few days or even longer, but the use of waterwheels to power machines invariably meant chaos as one part of a long process stopped. Streams that were known to never dry up became very valuable assets and on some there would be dozens of mills following the stream's journey down a valley.

Before the 1500s the second most common use after grinding corn was in the fulling of woollen cloth. This process involved pounding the woollen cloth in water, originally done by hand using a wooden beam or plank. In the waterwheel version, large hammers were lifted by cams on a rotating shaft and released to drop onto the cloth, which sat in a water-filled wooden box along with fuller's earth. This process filled out the woven cloth and gave it body. Any pre-1700 reference to waterwheels being used in the woollen industries only relates to the fulling process.

During the 16th century, waterwheels started to find other industrial roles. They were used in lead and copper mines for pumping, by means of bucket and chain systems; for grinding and crushing mineral ores; and the most important use in our story, driving air bellows and drop hammers in the iron industries, as we shall see in the next chapter.

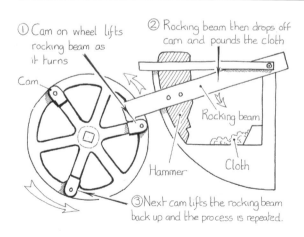

① Cam on wheel lifts rocking beam as it turns

② Rocking beam then drops off cam and pounds the cloth

Cam

Rocking beam

Hammer

Cloth

③ Next cam lifts the rocking beam back up and the process is repeated.

FIG 3.15: *Fulling stocks. For centuries woven woollen cloth was pounded, or fulled, using waterwheel-driven hammers. Usually a pair of hammers were mounted side by side, and dropped alternately causing the cloth to turn. Very few examples still exist, though an excellent fulling stock can be seen at the Helmshore Mills Textile Museum.*

FIG 3.16: *Sheffield Industrial Museums Trust, part of the Abbeydale Industrial Hamlet site, with one of the three waterwheels just visible.*

FIG 3.17: *Cheddleton Mill, showing the leat and both wheels.*

CHAPTER 4

Materials
of Our Dreams

FIG 4.1: *The classic symbol of the Industrial Revolution. This is the cast iron bridge that spans the river Severn at Ironbridge, erected in 1779 by Abraham Darby's grandson. Though it almost bankrupted the builder, it became the first statement worldwide of what could be done with iron. Held together by mortised joints and wedges, (it predated the arrival of reliable nuts and bolts), it substituted metal for wood but looks like a giant demonstration of woodworking techniques.*

Iron

Iron is probably the most important material made by man. It exists in three broad types: wrought iron, cast (or pig) iron and the steels. To extract iron from its ore, it has to be heated. Early work used a charcoal fire in a crude oven – the bloomery furnace – which made an equally crude iron rich cake. This had to be beaten to separate the iron from the slag. Lime was added to the mix and acted as a flux, allowing the iron to separate more easily and to form at a slightly lower temperature. The process was improved by using bellows to drive air through the burning charcoal to generate a higher temperature, giving a quicker conversion and better separation of the slag. This furnace produced a very pure form called wrought iron. By reheating, but not melting, wrought iron can be shaped. It is strong in tension and lasts a very long time. It also possesses the ability to be welded simply by beating red-hot iron together.

In the late 1400s a new 'blast' furnace had been developed in Belgium which produced much greater quantities of molten iron. Quickly taken up in England, the secret of this furnace was the use of large waterwheel-driven bellows to provide a vigorous air blast. The iron was now hot enough to run out of the furnace as a liquid, which was directed into a network of sand troughs to solidify. Someone thought these troughs bore a vague similarity to a sow with her young suckling, and the term pig iron was born. I will refer to the iron from these blast furnaces as 'pig iron' but use the term 'cast iron' when the iron is re-melted and poured into moulds. As the furnaces grew in size, bigger and bigger waterwheels and eventually steam engines were needed to drive the ever-growing bellows. The early blast furnaces used charcoal for the fuel as it burnt relatively cleanly and

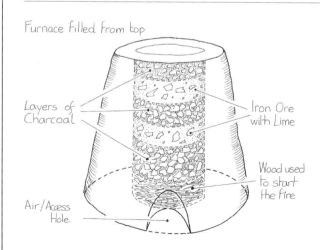

Furnace filled from top

Layers of Charcoal

Iron Ore with Lime

Wood used to start the fire

Air/Access Hole

FIG 4.2: *The bloomery furnace built from brick or stone and lined with a fireproof clay. Used from the earliest times to make small quantities of wrought iron, these furnaces were still in use in rural parts of India as recently as the 1960s.*

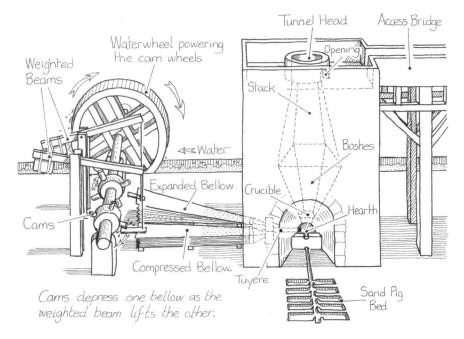

Weighted Beams

Waterwheel powering the cam wheels

Tunnel Head

Access Bridge

Opening

Stack

Water

Boshes

Expanded Bellow

Crucible

Cams

Hearth

Compressed Bellow.

Tuyere

Sand Pig Bed

Cams depress one bellow as the weighted beam lifts the other.

FIG 4.3: *The blast furnace, a development of the bloomery furnace built to a much larger scale. Due to good insulation and a powerful air blast, the furnace gets hot enough to make the iron molten. The tap hole at the base is plugged with clay until the iron is judged ready, when the plug is broken out and the molten iron flows freely into the prepared sand bed. The sand bed was usually under cover though many of today's remains have lost all trace of both the waterwheels and the sand beds. The slag that floats on top of the iron is removed last before the furnace is reloaded.*

provided the carbon needed to combine with the oxygen in the ore.

Originally centred in Kent, where rich deposits of good iron ore were found and where forests provided the wood for the charcoal, the industry later spread to South Wales and Yorkshire. Limestone remained a vital ingredient as a flux as it helped separate the iron from the slag and also reduced the temperature needed to complete the conversion. A typical charge for a small furnace would be 200 kg of iron ore, 100 kg of charcoal and 20 kg of limestone, which would make about 100 kg of iron. In the 1820s blast furnaces were blown with hot rather than cold air, which increased their efficiency even further and this has become standard practice.

Pig iron, however, still contains some carbon. It is brittle and cannot be forged

FIG 4.4: *Moira blast furnace in Leicestershire is an odd relic, having been built fairly late in the story around 1800. The high hopes, however, were not fulfilled and it closed after barely 10 years' use. The materials were brought through the top of the building behind, where they could be stored and measured out prior to being tipped into the top of the furnace.*

into useful shapes. The only objects made from it initially were cannon balls and firebacks.

The new blast furnace process, however, produced much greater quantities of iron than the old bloomery furnaces and the problem was now to convert the pig iron into the more useful wrought iron.

This was done by re-melting the pig iron in a finery, which was rather like a blacksmith's forge. The finer was a skilled man who had to judge the softness of the iron and not let it liquefy. At the appropriate time, the soft iron would be lifted from the finery and hammered to release more carbon and impurities. This heating and beating process would be repeated until the finer judged the iron to be pure wrought iron. The resultant mass of iron was then hammered into blocks, which could be transported to rolling mills or a forge. Here the block would be reheated enough to make it malleable and then shaped into the desired form. All this hammering was provided by hand for small items but as the products got larger, bigger hammers were needed. Thus, the waterwheel-driven

FIG 4.5: *Waterwheel-driven tilt hammers in the Abbeydale Industrial Hamlet near Sheffield. These were used to hammer a sandwich of wrought iron and a central bar of crucible steel to make crown scythe blades.*

tilt hammer was developed. The wheel turned various forms of cams, or trips, which lifted the hammer and then let it drop free. The speed of these hammers is quite breathtaking, and some could be worked at up to six blows per second.

We must now take up another thread in the story of iron. Abraham Darby came from a Quaker iron-making family in Birmingham but wanted to start making brass, which was much in demand. He moved to Bristol, then the centre for tin, copper and brass making, in 1699 and by 1704 he had established the Baptist Mills brass works producing brass ingots and wire. Solid brass objects were cast, that is molten brass was poured into moulds and allowed to set. The mould was then broken to release the casting and the sand reused to make a new mould. Darby wondered if this technique could be applied to iron to make better castings but the Dutch brass workers he employed couldn't solve the problems. However, a smart young apprentice, John Thomas, managed it in 1707 and Darby immediately bound Thomas in Articles to keep the secret for three years. They had used pig iron brought from South Wales but Darby wanted to control the entire process and looked for a suitable location. In 1708, he moved up the

Severn valley to Coalbrookdale, where relatives had advised of good deposits of iron ore (the Shropshire coal fields were then among the largest in Europe).

Throughout the first year, Darby worked on the problem of replacing charcoal with the much cheaper local coal. Iron ore readily takes up sulphur, which is contained in coal, resulting in a useless iron. By partly burning coal in open heaps, Darby found he could remove the sulphur, leaving the clean burning 'coke' that was to become the main fuel in the iron and steel industries. Strangely, Darby didn't

patent his new process. Patents not only required the process to be drawn up and explained but they also added a sense of approval to a new idea. The lack of a patent slowed down the spread of the coke process, which took over 20 years to be generally accepted in the iron trade.

Darby was now using his perfected casting techniques to produce a vast range of iron goods. Everything you could imagine was attempted: bridge sections, gear wheels, tables, chairs, fancy fences and gates, statues and pseudo bronze castings. His iron-

FIG 4.6: *Pride of place in the Coalbrookdale Museum of Iron is this table, cast entirely in iron, including the dogs.*

FIG 4.7: *Early cast iron cannon on display in Charlestown, Cornwall.*

FIG 4.8: *A 1762 cast iron fireback on display in the Dean Heritage Museum in Soudley, Gloucestershire (on loan from the Horniman Museum, London).*

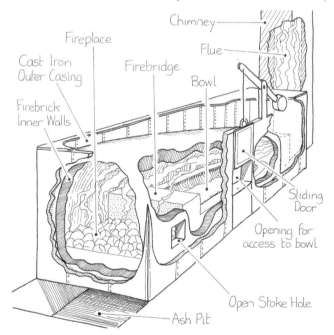

FIG 4.9: *The reverberatory furnace was made in many forms to serve the lead, brass and glass industries as well as iron. Examples still exist (normally just called puddling furnaces) including an occasionally fired one in the Blists Hill Museum, Ironbridge. Later developments using a cast iron bowl with cinders or mill scale as a layer of oxidising materials improved the process still further.*

making venture was a huge success; indeed the Ironbridge works still cast the Aga and Rayburn cookers to this day. The bridge across the river Severn (erected by his grandson in 1779) stands as a memorial to the iron casting skills of his works.

Due mainly to government alarm at the rate at which charcoal making was destroying our forests, the glass industry had been ordered to stop using charcoal back in 1610 (lead and brass industries followed around 1680). A new type of furnace that could use coal as the fuel – called a reverberatory furnace – was thus developed for these industries. The coal fire is kept separate from the melting metal, which receives its heat from the hot flue gases aided by reflected heat from the brick tunnel it sits in. First applied to ironwork in 1784 by Henry Cort, it could convert much larger quantities of pig iron than the old finery furnace, thus satisfying the ever-growing demand for wrought iron.

The pig iron is placed in a bowl (sand on firebricks) and the oxygen needed to convert the pig iron to wrought iron is provided by the draught caused by using a chimney to draw the fire. A

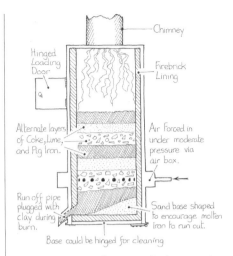

FIG 4.10: *A modern cupola furnace, in practice a simplified blast furnace. Early versions were built in fireclay-lined brick but the principle was the same.*

facility is made to allow the molten iron to be stirred, thus allowing more of the iron to be exposed to the oxygen which gave rise to the term 'puddling'.

Freed from their need for charcoal, the iron making centres now settled near to the sources of coal and the old charcoal based areas began to fade. Pig iron was dispatched to foundries

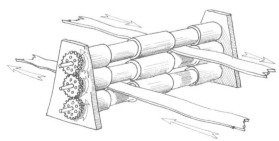

FIG 4.11: *A 'three high' rolling mill. Men would stand both sides, passing the iron to and fro between the rollers. The gaps between the rollers were arranged to be progressively smaller, each pass slowly reducing the thickness until the final size was achieved.*

FIG 4.12: *The steam hammer, built in an amazing range of sizes, became the mainstay of the forging industry. This depiction of a flat bar being shaped is in the Sheffield Industrial Museums Trust, Kelham Island Museum in Sheffield. When large steam hammers were in use, everyone in the town knew, as the thud would resound throughout the surrounding area.*

throughout the country where yet another new furnace, the cupola, had arrived, making the reheating of the iron easier and cheaper. Casting could now be done almost anywhere, indeed the cupola furnace is still made today for small quantity or hobby use.

Hammering wrought iron into everyday shapes like flat strips and round shafts took time and skill, so creative minds had invented the slitting mill. This arrived as early as 1590 and heralded the start of new ways of working wrought iron into the forms needed by industry. The slitting mill

was used to cut or slit iron, which had been beaten into a flat bar, to a fixed width even though the thickness might be a bit uneven. This flat bar was used for the rims of cartwheels plus many tasks like straps and barrel bands. Later, the slitting mill was developed into the rolling mill where the hot wrought iron was passed through shaped rollers turned, yet again, by waterwheels. Great strength and skill was needed as the red-hot iron bars were steered into and out of the rollers using just long tongs. This process enabled linear shapes to be made:

strips, rods and eventually flat sheets.

It is interesting to note that, as late as 1720, Britain still imported over 60% of its pig iron but, by the 1780s, iron was being exported. By the 1830s, we were producing great quantities of pig iron, some re-melted for casting into all manner of items, including many that were useful for engineering and construction. The rest was converted into wrought iron, which could be rolled into a vast range of strips, angles and flat sheets. A small quantity went to the traditional wrought iron trades such as chain and nail making.

Wrought iron had been worked by hand hammering, followed by waterwheel-driven trip and helm hammers, but there were limits to how large an object could be forged. When Brunel was planning the SS *Great Britain*, the original idea had been to use paddle wheels and for these he needed a wrought iron shaft of massive dimensions (a diameter of about 30 inches). Around 1839 James Nasmyth developed a new kind of hammer to meet Brunel's needs – the steam hammer. This raised a large weight vertically and allowed it to drop in a controlled manner. Because the weight was carried in guides, the blows it delivered were consistent and immense. In the event, Brunel used the newly invented propeller but the use of the steam hammer spread as the means of forging large items in iron and steel.

Later, the power of steam was used not just to raise the hammer but also to drive it down. This not only increased

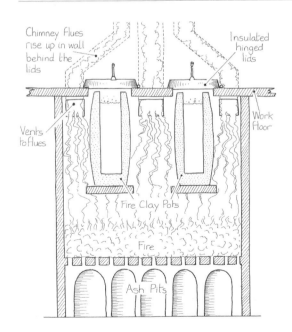

Chimney Flues rise up in wall behind the lids

Insulated hinged lids

Vents to flues

Work Floor

Fire Clay Pots

Fire

Ash Pits

FIG 4.13: *Diagram showing how the crucible pots were heated. The blister steel was heated to around 1550°C for 3 to 4 hours. Great strength and judgement were needed to lift and manoeuvre the red hot pots. Still held in long handled tongs the molten steel was poured into moulds (called teeming). This was a very tricky operation, as the moulds had to be filled without splashing the molten steel onto the sides, thus producing a clean ingot free from air pockets. (Steel, see page 42)*

FIG 4.14: *Crucible furnaces at the Abbeydale Industrial Hamlet. Note the long handled tongs used to hold and lift the pots.*

the force in each blow but it could now be controlled.

Steel

Steel is basically a form of wrought iron with a very accurate percentage of carbon – 1% to 2% – compared to wrought iron with less than 1% or pig iron at over 4%. Steel had been produced in very small quantities from the 1200s by packing strips of wrought iron between layers of charcoal in a cementation furnace for around two to three weeks. This caused the carbon from the charcoal to migrate into the surface of the iron. Blister steel, so called because of the surface appearance, was then reheated and hammered to mix the blisters of carbonised iron into the rest of the iron, producing shear steel. This steel gave a good cutting edge and was used to make sheep shears as well as weapons. In 1740, this method was improved by an English clock maker, Benjamin Huntsman, who was seeking a better steel to make clock springs. By employing the new crucible furnace, he was able to melt the blister steel completely, which in its liquid state allowed the carbon to redistribute itself evenly throughout the iron. He also perfected adding other elements to produce a range of steels including, of course, spring steel and he did it just outside Sheffield. This area was blessed with fast-flowing streams with which to drive waterwheels, used to power bellows for the furnaces and hammers to shape the metal. The presence of millstone grit in the same area also made grinding and shaping the steel easy, hence the start of the cutlery trade in this part of the country. For the next 100 years, the Sheffield region produced most of the world's best quality steel, indeed cementation furnaces were still in use into the 20th century.

The next breakthrough came in 1856 when Henry Bessemer developed the converter that bears his name whilst trying to improve wrought iron to make better gun barrels. The converter is a brick-lined retort into which molten pig iron is poured. Under considerable pressure, air is then forced into the base of the retort and thus up through

FIG 4.15: *A grinding horse and stone used to sharpen scythe blades at the Abbeydale Industrial Hamlet. The operator sat astride the machine, leant forward and sharpened the blade on the revolving stone. This type of work in the Sheffield area had a terrible reputation for ill health and injuries.*

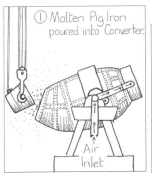
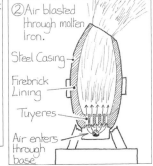

① Molten Pig Iron poured into Converter.

② Air blasted through molten Iron.

Steel Casing

Firebrick Lining

Tuyeres

Air enters through base

Air Inlet

③ Molten Steel poured out.

FIG 4.16: *The Bessemer process. These converters form a popular visual image in steel making, being very large, dramatic and emitting masses of sparks and smoke.*

the molten iron. The carbon in the iron is obviously very hot but, being trapped within the iron, has no oxygen. Injecting the air now provides the carbon with air, which then burns furiously within the molten mass and produces carbon dioxide, which erupts along with the unused air from the top of the retort. Rather than cool the iron the effect of the carbon burning actually increases the temperature of the iron mass in the converter and thus the process needs no external energy or fuel. After only 30 minutes the carbon content is reduced to the level needed, judged, incidentally, by the colour of

FIG 4.17: *A Bessemer converter proudly standing at the entrance to the Kelham Island Museum. The air pipe entered at the left, whilst the gearing to the right tipped the converter.*

the sparks erupting from the top. The retort is then tipped and the molten steel is poured into ingots, which are then taken for rolling or casting. The cost of steel dropped from £50 a ton in 1850 to just £4 a ton twenty years later.

The early converters produced some 10 cwt of steel in just 30 minutes but very soon converters to handle up to 30 tons at a time were in use. Because the converter could pour all its contents out in one go, very large steel castings became possible. The best steel was made from low phosphoric ores such as those from the Barrow-in-Furness area and Spain. Small amounts of manganese added to the molten mass were found to reduce brittleness and this was only the beginning of experimentation that produced a wide range of steels. One of the first mass uses of steel was for railway track. Steel has the useful property of hardening with use, ideal for rail track. The quantity of steel produced was quite staggering, with Sheffield manufacturing more rails between 1865 and 1874 than anywhere else in the world. Some 175,000 miles of rail were exported to America alone!

Steel slowly and surely replaced wrought iron until, by 1976, wrought iron production had ceased in England.

FIG 4.18: *Forge Mill is an example of a specialised application of iron and steel. Redditch had become the centre for making needles, just as its neighbour Bromsgrove had become the centre for nails. Needles were made in small home workshops and were then brought to Forge Mill to be polished. This process involved thousands of needles being packed into trays, which were rocked to and fro by giant waterwheel-driven cranks.*

CHAPTER 5

Power of a
Thousand Horses

The steam engine belongs entirely to the Industrial Revolution, whereas all the other subjects we are discussing existed before 1750 and were simply improved by it.

Mining had a problem, a serious problem: the depth a miner could reach was limited by the presence of water, which flooded the workings. It is certain that many people had pondered possible solutions. However, as with so many developments, it is the best solution that wins, the others simply fading into the background of history. So it was with the pumping of water from mines, though the machine to do it had an effect on life way beyond the expectations of its inventor.

In 1606, the philosopher Porta of Naples had described two experiments in which he had demonstrated that steam could be used to push water from a tank and that steam, when condensed back to water, would create a partial vacuum (steam occupies over 1,500 times the volume of the water it comes from). In 1641, the Duke of Tuscany managed to raise water by suction but he could never exceed a lift of 28 ft (8.5 m), a figure that intrigued the Italian physician and mathematician, Evangelista Torricelli, who experimented and eventually

worked out that the atmosphere had weight and that this air pressure was the force involved in combating a vacuum, not the vacuum itself.

Around 1690, in Cornwall, Thomas Savery had built a steam-driven pump in an attempt to solve the flooding of the mines. The pump employed condensing steam to draw water up into a receiver and then, having changed over the necessary valves, it used steam to push the water further up. This pressure phase was the machine's downfall; it was rarely able to manage more than a few feet due to the limitations of the ironwork of the time.

The engine itself was not a success and it was never used in mines, but Savery had obtained patents for 'raising water by the impellant force of fire' – a classification so broad that it covered almost everything relating to steam pumps.

Thomas Newcomen, then working as an ironmonger in Dartmouth, came across a failed Savery engine. While he was working on it, the accidental rapid cooling of the steam collapsed the cylinder with such force that the engine was wrecked. Newcomen realised that this rapid cooling down of hot steam had produced an immense force. He soon developed his own ideas

FIG 5.1: *The Savery engine was in fact quite clever – it failed due to the limitations of the ironwork of the day. The operation, always performed by hand, was as follows. Starting with all the valves closed, open valve A to admit steam to the cylinder then close A. Next open C and B to drench the cylinder in cold water. This cooling produces a partial vacuum in the cylinder, which draws water up via valve C into the cylinder. Now close C and then open A and D. The idea was that the steam pressure would push the water from the cylinder and up the exit pipe. The problem was always this pressure phase – the pipework was never strong enough to withstand more than just 2 or 3 pounds per square inch pressure, which could only lift the water 4 to 5 ft (1.5 m).*

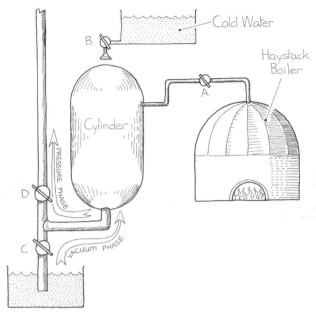

to use this vacuum to pull down a piston but, in order to avoid problems with patents, he went into partnership with Savery and the Newcomen atmospheric engine was born. Though often associated with the Cornish mines, the first machine was in fact erected to lift water from a coalmine in Dudley, near Birmingham, in 1712. Rated at around 5.5 hp, the pumps it operated lifted 10 gallons of water 153 ft with each stroke of the beam – some 5,000 gallons an hour.

In this process, steam at a very low pressure is allowed to fill the cylinder. The inlet valve is then closed and a jet of cold water is injected directly into the steam in the cylinder. This causes the steam to condense into water and thus create a vacuum beneath the piston, which, pushed by the natural atmospheric pressure we all live in, is driven down. This single power stroke is used to pull down one end of a rocking beam; the other end, now rising, lifts a rod, which descends down the mine shaft. In the shaft is a series of pumps worked by this upward stroke of the pump rod.

Next, the condensed steam and cooling water has to be drained from the cylinder, the drain is then closed,

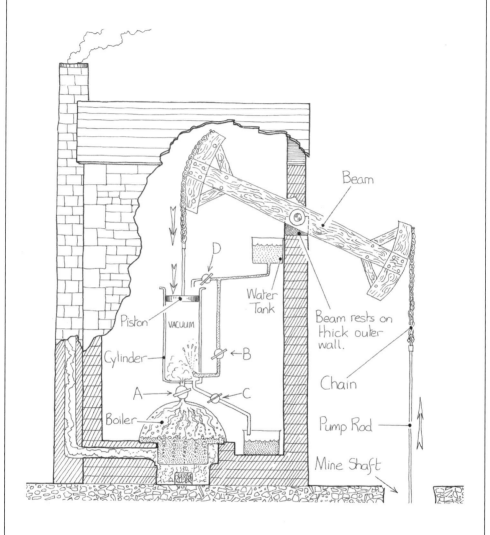

FIG 5.2: *The basic features of the original Newcomen engine. First admit steam to the cylinder via valve A. Next condense the steam by opening B to produce a spray of cold water into the cylinder. The natural air pressure forces the piston down producing the power stroke, raising the outside end of the beam and the pump rod going down the mine shaft. Valve B is closed and valve C is opened to drain out the condensed steam and air. The weight of the pump rod now pulls the beam back down thus raising the piston. Valve D allows water to be run onto the top of the piston to aid in maintaining a good seal against the rough surface of the cylinder walls.*

FIG 5.3: *The pump end of the beam, showing the arc and the chain used to keep the rod moving in a straight line. This reconstruction of an early Newcomen engine is in the Black Country Living Museum – within a mile of where the first engine was erected back in 1712.*

after which the steam pipe can be opened allowing the piston to rise up by the simple weight of the mine rod and the pumps pulling the beam down. The cycle is then repeated.

The main difficulty with any beam engine is that the piston needs to travel in a straight line to keep a good seal and not jam in the cylinder, but the end of the beam to which it is attached describes an arc, so a solution had to be found. As these early engines only pulled the beam down, a delightful arrangement was devised, where the end of the beam carried a curved channel in which a chain ran and dropped down to connect to the piston. The same solution was used at

the other end of the beam for the pump rod going down the mine. The weight of the pump rod and power stroke from the cylinder kept the chains in tension.

With power only produced on the downward stroke of the piston and just the pump rod weight to look after the upward stroke, the motion of these engines is rather jerky and the timing of the water injection is critical. As no rotating motion is involved there is no way to use a flywheel to smooth out the motion. The early engines, like Savery's, were operated completely by hand; that they achieved twelve strokes a minute for hours on end is amazing.

Soon, though, Newcomen devised a way to operate the various valves automatically, using power from the beam. It was estimated that two men driving a Newcomen engine could raise as much water in 24 hours as had previously needed 20 men with 50 horses working non-stop for 3½ days.

Within ten years, these engines were in use all over England and even in Europe. The steam engine had arrived. It was the first serious source of power that could be built where it was needed and not where nature happened to provide a river. There was a catch, though, (there always is!). The engines consumed vast quantities of coal, and coal was heavy and difficult to move over land. When used to drain coalmines this obviously didn't matter, and even the Cornish tin and lead mines were near the sea where Welsh coal could be brought to shore, albeit incurring import duty! But these engines were not economical unless the coal supply was easy. Various engineers made minor improvements, which helped, but they still remained inefficient.

Our story now moves to Glasgow in 1769, (some say 1764), where one James Watt was working in the university as an instrument maker. He was asked to repair a working model of a Newcomen engine, which had broken down. He naturally studied the workings in order to effect the repair and in doing so he realised that the engine was fundamentally inefficient. During the next five years he redesigned the way the steam was condensed to produce a more efficient engine. Watt had realised that the use of water to cool the steam within the

cylinder also cooled the cylinder walls. Thus, as fresh steam entered the cylinder, it immediately started to condense, wasting time and energy.

By separating the engine cylinder and the condensing vessel, the cylinder could be kept hot and the cooling vessel kept cold – opening the valve joining the two now instigated the power stroke. Watt's next improvement was to close the top of the cylinder and as the condensing action was pulling the piston down, steam was admitted above the piston to also push the piston down. Though still using low steam pressures – Watt never used pressures above 5 pounds per square inch (0.34 bar) – this extra energy improved the engine's efficiency even further. During the upward stroke, still powered by the weight of the pump rods, the steam above the piston was passed down a pipe (called the equaliser pipe) to fill the cylinder below the piston ready for the condensing phase.

Yet again we have parallel activities, on the main

The early engines had used brass for the cylinders but, as bigger engines were demanded, the cost of the brass became prohibitive. It is now 1772 and our story rejoins Abraham Darby, whose expertise in iron casting helped Watt to develop larger cast iron cylinders for ever bigger engines. But they were still not good enough to make a really effective seal between the piston and the rough wall of the cast cylinder or

At virtually the same time, in Bersham near Wrexham, two brothers,

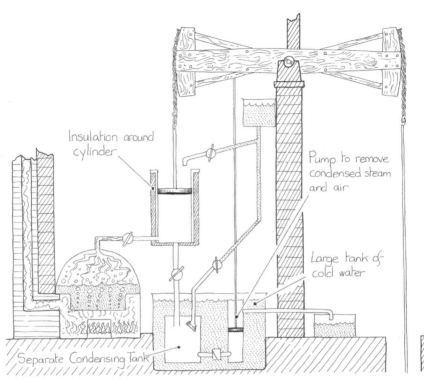

FIG 5.4: *Watt's first improvement was to use a separate condensing tank, which sat in a larger open tank of cold water. He insulated the cylinder, which now stayed hot at all times. He added a pump to remove the condensed water and air, and thanks to the better ironwork he raised the operating pressure to a cautious 5 pounds per square inch.*

John and William Wilkinson, operated an iron foundry and had been approached by the French government to produce a more efficient cannon. The French cannon were notorious for exploding when fired. Apart from using better iron and casting techniques, John designed a machine, driven by an early Watt steam engine (one of the first two engines produced by Boulton & Watt with a 38 inch (1.1 m) cylinder), to bore an accurate hole through the cast barrel. This development solved Watt's last problem – the provision of a straight and true tube for his engine cylinder, allowing a much better fitting piston and rod and in the much cheaper material, iron.

Watt also improved the condenser itself, using a water tank positioned above the engine to give pressure to the

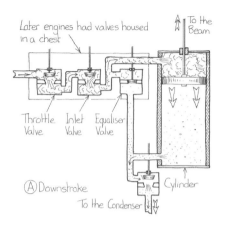
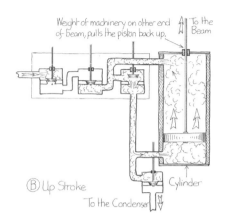

FIG 5.5: *Watt's next improvements – (left) closing the top of the cylinder to add steam pressure to the downward 'condensing' stroke, then (right) this steam was transferred to below the piston, ready for the next power stroke.*

cold water jet plus a better injector. He then added a separate pump, still driven from the beam, which removed the warm condensed water plus any air from the condenser. The warm water was then used as the feed for the boiler, again reducing the heating needed. All these small but significant improvements added up to an amazing reduction in fuel consumption – only a quarter of the coal used by the Newcomen engine with the same power.

We can now sense that there are several interlinked events that need to be accurately timed for all this to work and, indeed, if we look at these early engines, we will see the array of rods and cams that control the various valves.

Watt also adapted the centrifugal governor, first used in flour grinding mills, to control the engine speed as the load varied.

There is an amusing but by no means unique story of Darby's iron works in Coalbrookdale. Originally a series of eight waterwheels were installed running down the side of the hill, all used to power bellows for blast furnaces. The problem was that the water supply sometimes ran dry in summer and work would have to stop. The first solution was to employ a horse-driven water pump to return water from the bottom of the flight back up to the top. A Newcomen engine took over the task, later to be replaced by a Watt engine. The thought of using a steam engine to keep waterwheels running seems odd but, of course, it was the cheapest solution to a seasonal problem. Later still, massive steam-driven air pumps took over and the waterwheels all but vanished – the waterwheel sites can still be made out, but only just!

FIG 5.6: *The cylinder of a James Watt engine of 1779 built to pump water around the Smethwick locks on the Birmingham Canal network – a proud centrepiece in the Thinktank museum in Birmingham. The various valves are operated by the rod on the right, which is attached to the beam out of sight above the picture. The large square pipe is the equaliser pipe, which transferred the steam from above the piston to below it. This engine could raise 18,000 tonnes of water per day.*

Watt's next step forward was to adapt the engine to produce rotary motion. By using a heavy flywheel it would be possible to use the downward vacuum stroke to start the rotation, allowing the flywheel to complete the cycle just as the heavy pump rod did in the mines. However, few, including Watt, thought that the jerky motion of the engine could ever be coupled to a flywheel. Nevertheless, some engineers did just that and, whilst not perfect, these engines produced rotating motion from a steam engine for the first time. In particular, Matthew Wasborough had

done just this at a button factory in Birmingham owned by James Pickard, and to Watt's annoyance they had patented the system.

Watt also produced a truly double-acting engine in which the upward stroke was powered by condensing the steam above the piston; in effect, the downward stroke simply inverted. Having power on both the upward and downward stroke would provide a much smoother action, more practical for driving a flywheel to give rotating power. One problem, though, was that the old chain connection to the

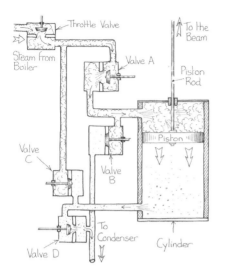
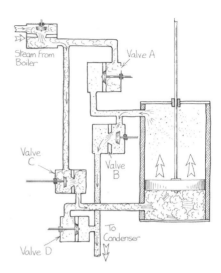

FIG 5.7: *Watt's double-acting engine. This engine operates like a normal Watt engine for the downward stroke (left) but then operates upside down for the upward stroke (right). Both strokes are now virtually identical in terms of the power applied to the beam.*

beam wouldn't work; you can't push with a chain!

Watt then developed what he thought was his finest invention: a system of solid links that would keep the piston rod moving in a straight line, but being solid links they could push and pull.

The last step was to convert the nodding beam to produce rotation. The obvious way is to use the crank – like pedalling a bicycle – but until 1791 when Wasborough and Pickard's patent ran out, Watt used a sun and planet gear (see fig 5.9).

From the very start, Watt had teamed up with Matthew Boulton to manufacture his engines, and the Boulton & Watt factory in Birmingham produced some 500 engines in the first 25 years, of which 52 were recorded as being used in mines, 84 in cotton mills and the rest, some 364 machines, were used in a variety of other manufacturing industries. Over half of these machines produced a rotating motion. With higher coal production and thanks to the canals, easy coal transportation, machine-driven power was now available almost anywhere it was needed. It was now 1800 and the revolution had truly begun.

It is interesting to note that, despite its widespread use, nobody had apparently sought to improve or adapt the Newcomen engine. James Watt had not set out to develop an engine and indeed his involvement came 40 years

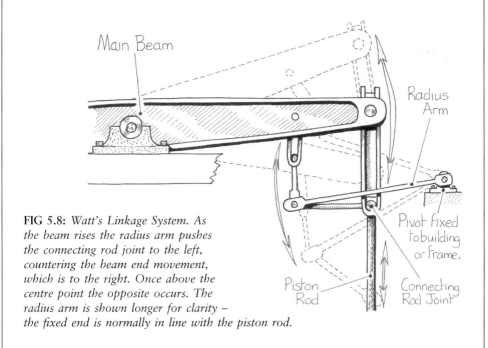

FIG 5.8: *Watt's Linkage System. As the beam rises the radius arm pushes the connecting rod joint to the left, countering the beam end movement, which is to the right. Once above the centre point the opposite occurs. The radius arm is shown longer for clarity – the fixed end is normally in line with the piston rod.*

FIG 5.9: *This scale model, in the Derby Industrial Museum, neatly shows the sun and planet gears at the end of the crank rod. The left hand gear is fixed to the crank arm whilst the right hand gear is fixed to the shaft. The two gears are kept in mesh by a tie bar.*

FIG 5.10: *The piston end of the mighty Samson blast furnace air pump, now standing in the Blists Hill Museum in Ironbridge. Watt's linkage system can be seen above the classical style decoration of the valve chest.*

after the first Newcomen engines were built. That he had the foresight to realise the potential marked him out as one of the new breed of engineering entrepreneurs.

The force available in the condensing stroke is limited by the air pressure, approximately 15 pounds per square inch. By 1800, though, improved ironwork and boiler developments had allowed much higher steam pressures to be generated and it was now possible to drop the condensing cycle altogether and rely only on the force of the steam to push the piston up and down. This use of higher pressure steam also meant that, for the same output power, the engine could be made physically smaller.

Before we look at the steady engine improvements to come, let's examine the pumps that these early engines had been made to drive.

There were two basic types: lift pumps and force pumps. Both types are also known by several other names. They both use flap valves to allow water to be drawn upwards and prevented from returning downwards. The lift pumps do their work on the upward stroke of the pump rod, whereas the force pumps use the weight of the pump rods to do the work, with the engine using its energy to lift the pump rod back up.

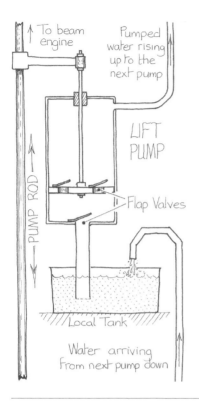

↑ To beam engine

Pumped water rising up to the next pump

LIFT PUMP

Flap Valves

← PUMP ROD →

Local Tank

Water arriving from next pump down

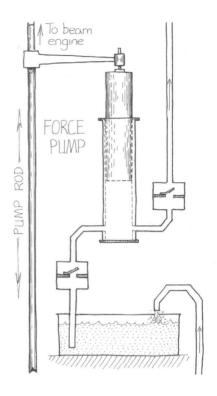

↑ To beam engine

FORCE PUMP

← PUMP ROD →

In 1800 Watt's patents ran out and fresh minds looked again at the steam engine. One such was Richard Trevithick who experimented with higher pressure engines and took the imaginative step of using engines to power moving machines. His first steam-powered road vehicle was tried out in 1801 but the roads simply weren't good enough. He turned his attention to rails and his first railway engine was built in 1803. Watt had always resisted any move to use his machines in this way.

It had taken just 100 years from the first pump engines until steam could

FIG 5.11: *The lift pump (above left) and the force pump (above right) were stacked every 70 ft (21 m) or so down the mine shaft. Often a side tunnel (slough) would be cut to take the water away to lower ground. These could be several miles long but were worth the effort as it saved raising the water any further.*

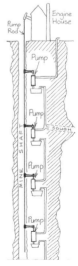

FIG 5.12: *A small single cylinder beam engine driving a flywheel to provide rotating motion. This type of engine became the workhorse for smaller industries around the turn of the 1800s. This one is on show in the Dean Heritage Museum and like so many engines has undergone modification – the piston coupling and valve gear being much later than the rest of the engine.*

FIG 5.13: *This working replica of one of Trevithick's early engines is in the Blists Hill Museum, Ironbridge. The engine ran on the old flanged rails of the early tramways.*

power almost anything that moved!

During this period, improvements were taking place in all the industrial activities, often one area benefiting from advances in another only to return the compliment by aiding further improvement in the first area.

In steam engines the most obvious changes were of scale. The slow ponderous pumping engines grew and grew until there were cylinders of awesome dimensions – diameters of over 6 ft (1.75 m) with piston strokes of over 10 ft (2.9 m) became common. The pumps they drove also expanded in size, helped by improved iron casting techniques and better metal working machines.

One area of development involved the valves that controlled the entry and exit of the steam from the cylinder. Several engineers patented valve systems that to this day carry their names. The early engines had used valves similar to those used in modern car engines – the bathplug.

These were lifted and lowered as needed but because of their very large diameters they had a problem when used with the higher steam pressures. To open the valve meant pulling against the pressure of the steam. On Cornish pumping engines this was solved by the double beat valve: the two valves are arranged in such a way that one is being pushed closed by the steam pressure whilst the other is being pushed open. By making the 'pushed closed' valve slightly bigger the valves stayed shut but needed much less work to open.

In 1799, William Murdock, chief erector for Boulton & Watt, designed the slide valve for use with rotating engines. There is no force to overcome

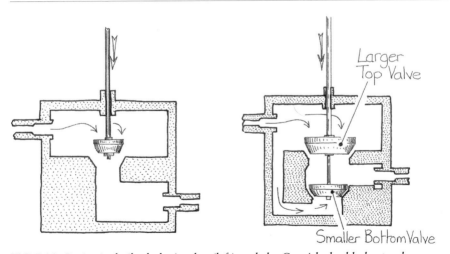

FIG 5.14: *Basic single 'bathplug' valve (left) and the Cornish double beat valve (right), which was designed to overcome the high pressure needed to open the single valve.*

(other than friction) and as it provides both the entry and exit valves in one unit, only one gland and operating rod is needed. The piston valve (as used on railway engines) uses a similar mechanism.

The Victorians produced some truly amazing steam engines, invariably highly decorated in that delightful over-the-top way that typifies the 1830–1880 period.

This is the same period that saw the steam engine become portable, not just to pull goods like a railway or steam lorry but to take power to where it was needed, usually in agriculture and, after the 1860s, to fairgrounds.

Though some waterwheels and windmills carried on into the 20th century, the steam engine powered virtually everything and until the diesel engine and the electric motor arrived it reigned supreme.

Steam ships had a unique problem. They had to carry all the coal and pure water needed for the entire journey and, if that was to be a long trip, then much of the ship would be taken up by fuel. Many thought it impossible to cross the Atlantic using just a steam engine since the ship couldn't carry enough coal and water. This drove the engineers to

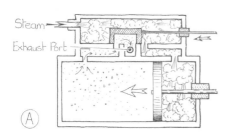

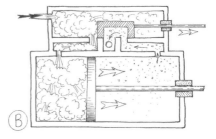

FIG 5.15: *Slide valve (above left and right) The 'U' shaped block slides to and fro, opening or closing the entrances to the cylinder. All steam engines only admit high pressure steam for a brief part of the stroke – the expansion of the steam completes the stroke. The piston valve (below left and right) works in a similar way but is easier to seal than the rectangular shape used in the slide valve.*

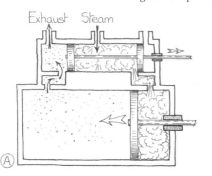

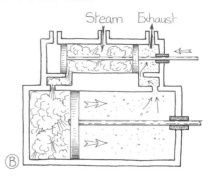

FIG 5.16: *Just part of the beautifully decorated sewage pumps erected in the Abbey Pumping Station to serve Leicester. There are four Woolf compound engines, installed in 1891 by Gimson & Co. Typical of Victorian engineering, this all reflected a true pride in their municipal works.*

FIG 5.17: *Just part of the valve operating gear on one of the enormous water pumping engines at the Kew Bridge Steam Museum. Compare this with the basic valve operating gear on the early Watt engine in Fig 5.6.*

FIG 5.18: *By 1835 railway engines were already taking on the shape we would recognise today. This fine replica of 'Planet' stands in the Museum of Science & Industry in Manchester.*

FIG 5.19: *The crank replaced the beam and along with the slide valve produced the true workhorse of the Victorian era. Manufactured in their thousands, this type of horizontal engine was made in every imaginable size. This one is used at the Black Country Living Museum as a winding engine.*

develop more efficient engines.

High pressure steam at, say, 150 pounds per square inch, enters the cylinder and pushes the piston. It is normal to shut the steam off before the piston reaches the end of its stroke, thus using the natural expansion of the steam to complete the stroke. The steam, though, is still at quite a high pressure and this energy gets wasted as exhaust. What the designers did was to reuse this exhaust steam by putting it into an accumulator vessel which, in turn, fed a lower pressure cylinder driving the same shaft as the first high pressure one. The diameter of the second cylinder was larger, to compensate for the lower pressure. This technique was used to develop triple and even quadruple expansion engines both for ships and for land use.

The final improvement was to condense the final exhaust steam back to water, which was reused in the boiler. The importance of this is that condensed steam produces very pure water, free from salts, which is essential to prevent both pipes and boilers from furring up. The most evident use of this technique today is the cooling towers seen alongside power stations, their job being simply to condense the exhausted

FIG 5.20: *A triple expansion engine from the excellent collection at the Kew Bridge Steam Museum. The expansion tanks are between the cylinders below the walkway.*

steam and return it as pure water for the boilers.

Though the very early Norse waterwheel had used the idea of a crude turbine, nothing further happened until the mid 1800s when the availability of iron and steel enabled the idea of a turbine to be reinvented. Replacing the waterwheel in mills and factories, a few can still be seen working today.

In 1884, Charles Parsons had patented the steam-driven turbine, originally developed to give higher speeds for generating electricity. To work with steam the flat rotating blades had now changed to long thin blades like a propeller or a fan.

Ignoring the ridicule and lack of interest in his turbines from the Admiralty, Parsons produced a dramatic demonstration in 1897 with his turbine-driven ship, the *Turbina*, which reached the unheard of speed of 34.5 knots. So impressed was the Admiralty and the shipbuilding industry in general that within just another ten years, the 38,000 ton *Mauritania* had reached 26 knots powered by its 70,000 hp turbines – over ten thousand times the power of Newcomen's first commercial engine 185 years earlier.

FIG 5.21: *Some of the most evocative machines restored for our pleasure are the portable steam engines. Equipped with winches and belt drive pulleys they could travel to almost any site to provide power.*

FIG 5.22: *A close relative to the portable steam engine is the even more decorated showman's engine. Their flamboyant appearance hides a well-engineered, hard-working piece of Victorian engineering.*

CHAPTER 6

Cloth for All

The textile industry is very old and little remains of the early centuries of work. However, there are many excellent reconstructed examples of textile manufacture from the 15th century and on through the machine age. It is perhaps the best represented application of mechanisation we have in our museums.

The basic process of making cloth applies to all materials except for felt. The raw material is selected for quality, washed and combed, before being drawn out to form a thread. This is spun to achieve strength and then woven on a loom to form cloth. Finally, the cloth is finished and dyed. The basic materials are flax, silk, wool and cotton.

Linen

Linen, made from flax fibres, is probably the oldest cloth made by man, with references going back at least 2,500 years. Flax (linseed) is a member of a group of plants that possess a remarkable feature. Just beneath the outer surface of the stems are bunches of fine fibres, which run the entire length of the plant, including the roots. There can be upwards of 1,000 fibres per stem and flax can be grown up to 4 ft high. Hemp is another such plant, which can grow to over 10 ft high and is used to make a coarser thread suitable for sacking and ropes. The plants, always including the roots, are harvested, dried and then the outer bark removed by retting. This involves rotting away the hard tissues to leave the fibres, which are then cleaned and combed (hackling) to produce bundles of fine fibres ready to be spun. Relatively little was made in England, most coming from Ireland, Scotland and Belgium. With flax, the bundle of fibres is held on a distaff above the spinning wheel, and the fibres are drawn down by hand to be twisted and wound onto bobbins. It is then woven into cloth in a way similar to wool or cotton.

Silk

The next oldest material is silk, always an expensive material destined for the rich. Silk is obtained from the cocoon woven by the caterpillar of the silk moth (Bombyx mori). Amazing as it seems, the thread is produced by the caterpillar as one long thread and the challenge is to find the end and unwind it again! Once unwound the silk filament is ready for the next stage.

Unlike wool or cotton the silk fibre doesn't need to be teased out – it is already a single filament – so groups of six to fifteen filaments are drawn together and twisted before being wound onto bobbins. This silk thread is woven on looms in the same basic way as wool or cotton.

FIG 6.1: *Delightful reconstruction of carding and spinning in the home environment, on show at the Helmshore Mills Textile Museum. The children are hand carding the wool, whilst the women are spinning it into a thread.*

Wool

The processing of wool is the oldest and most widespread of the textile industries in England. Wool from sheep is tightly knotted and very greasy and the first step is to remove the dirt and grease. This was originally done with stale urine (which breaks down to ammonia) but later, thankfully, by using detergents. Incidentally, a by-product of the process is lanolin, used in soaps and cosmetics. At this stage the wool is graded by its colour, quality and fibre length as for many years most wool has been made from a blend of differing qualities. The shorter fibres are used in woollen goods, including knitting, the longer threads being used to make worsted thread.

The cleaned wool is now drawn between wire brushes to get the fibres partially straightened out into a soft web. Called carding, this was originally done by hand but machines took over in the late 1700s.

Later in the mechanised process, two other machines were used to break up the lumps of wool and to remove any dirt left in it. These, like so many early machines, have lovely names: the devil and the scutcher.

Carding machines are amongst the largest and most complicated machines used in wool production. The wire hand

FIG 6.2: *A mechanised carding machine with one of the covers lifted, on show at the Cotswold Woollen Weavers. The rollers may look smooth but are in fact covered with fine wire bristles. Similar machines (called hoppers, scribblers, devils and scutchers) were used to get the knots and dirt out of the wool or cotton mass.*

brushes are now replaced by wide drums covered in short wire teeth, with the wool passing between stationary and rotating drums. There may be up to 80 such rollers and the wool will have travelled up to 75 ft in passing through just one machine. The resultant wool mass is collected together into a soft round rope, called roving, which is stored in tall barrels.

As mentioned, the very best wool is used to make worsted thread, the wool being combed rather than carded. This produces a finer, harder thread with much less fluffiness compared to basic wool thread and makes the very finest

cloth used for suits. Thought to have been introduced by Flemish weavers working in the Norfolk village of Worstead, this section of the woollen industry became centred in Bradford and Newtown in Wales. In contrast to worsted, threads destined for woollen goods can be made from poorer quality wool and can contain mixes of old wool and even rags.

The next stage is to produce a thread that can be woven. This originally involved using a distaff and spindle and then, later, a spinning wheel. Wool is a collection of separate fibres (as is cotton), pull them and they will quickly part. It's rather like cotton-wool – tease out a piece to make a soft rope, about the size of a finger, and then pull each end. Now try the same test, but first twist the cotton-wool 'rope'; this time it will not part. This twisting together of many strands or fibres is the task performed by spinning.

The woollen mass produced by the carding stage is too thick to just simply be twisted, it has to be teased out and then twisted. This process was done by hand, firstly drawing out the wool, then using the spinning wheel to twist the thread and lastly to wind the twisted thread onto a bobbin.

An early development of the basic spinning wheel used a 'thread maker', which performed the second and third operations in one go.

Weaving is the making of cloth from the woollen thread, using a loom.

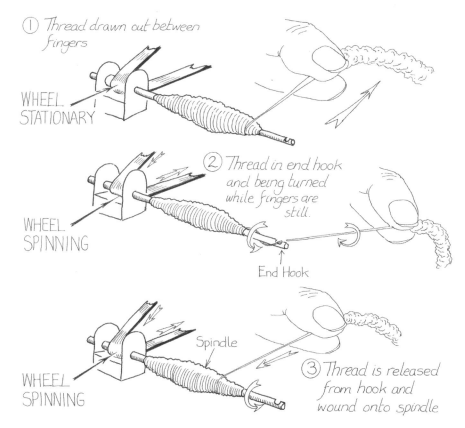

FIG 6.3: *The spinning wheel involves three distinct stages – unlike the Sleeping Beauty version! Each set of three moves makes about 12 inches (30 cm) of thread.*

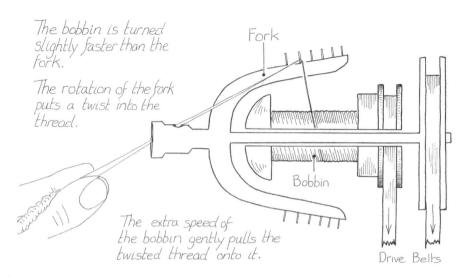

The bobbin is turned slightly faster than the fork.

The rotation of the fork puts a twist into the thread.

Fork

Bobbin

The extra speed of the bobbin gently pulls the twisted thread onto it.

Drive Belts

FIG 6.4 (above): *The first mechanisation. Here the twisting of the thread and the winding onto the bobbin are done by the thread maker. By turning the bobbin slightly faster than the fork (flyer), many twists are put into the thread for every turn wound onto the bobbin.*

FIG 6.5: *The thread maker as part of a spinning wheel. One of the interesting items in the collection held by the Carpet Museum Trust at their Weavers Loft museum in Kidderminster.*

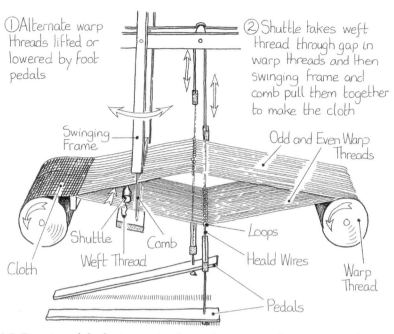

① Alternate warp threads lifted or lowered by foot pedals

② Shuttle takes weft thread through gap in warp threads and then swinging frame and comb pull them together to make the cloth

Swinging Frame

Odd and Even Warp Threads

Shuttle

Comb

Loops

Cloth

Weft Thread

Heald Wires

Warp Thread

Pedals

FIG 6.6: *Drawing of the basic weaving loom showing just those parts involved in the weaving.*

Though possessed of many variations, the basic principle is common to all weaving. Cloth consists of threads going side to side, called the weft, and threads running the length of the cloth, called the warp. The way the loom works is to have the warp threads prepared and wound onto drums. In silk this can be anything from 5,000 to 15,000 threads! Wool and cotton use mercifully less. The threads from the warp drum are individually pulled through eyes held on pull wires, called healds, before being passed through a fine comb (reed) and finally fixed across an empty take-up drum. The healds are organised in open wooden frames (shafts) which, for simplicity at this stage, we will limit to just two, one for the odd threads and one for all the even threads. The shafts are hung across the loom and are connected to the foot pedals in such a way that one board is above the other. By using the pedals the weaver can make the odd threads high and the even threads low, or vice versa. Parting the threads in this way leaves a gap between the two groups of thread called the shed. The weaver passes the weft thread from one side to the other through the shed. He then reverses the pedals and passes the weft thread back. This is repeated continuously, producing the weave.

This process, as described, would produce a very loose cloth so after each pass of the weft the weaver pulls the comb towards himself, packing the weft thread tight against the previous thread.

The weft thread is wound onto a small stick shaped to make it easy to pass from hand to hand. The width of the cloth, however, is limited to the distance the weaver can reach to pass the weft thread across the shed.

Finally, the cloth is washed and stretched to remove the last traces of grease and to let the woollen fibres relax and fill out. The washing phase involves placing the cloth in trays of water with fuller's earth and then beating it, a process called fulling. Originally done by treading the cloth with the feet, this was the first stage of the process that was taken over by machine – the fulling mill – using a waterwheel-driven set of hammers. The woollen cloth is then stretched out across two rows of tenter hooks to dry in the open and sometimes left out in sunshine to bleach. This is the origin of the phrase 'to be on tenterhooks'.

The wool industry was based on merchants who handled the raw wool and supplied the home-based weavers. Other merchants then organised the collection of the cloth and its eventual sale. The export of wool was of vital importance to the country, and the government of the day defended it at all costs. This protectionism, plus the local but widespread nature of the weaving process, produced a very entrenched industry, which fought off any attempts to improve or modernise it.

FIG 6.7: *Depiction of an early hand loom at the Helmshore Mills Textile Museum.*

We have now arrived in the 1700s and the textile revolution is about to start.

The story gets a little confusing at this stage as some of the early mechanisation was developed for the wool industry and quickly copied by the cotton weavers. Other machines were originally developed for the new upstart material, cotton, and soon taken up by the wool and silk industries though never on the same scale as cotton. I shall therefore switch to the story of cotton and follow that through the age of machines, bearing in mind that most of the mechanisation also applies to wool and silk.

Cotton

Cotton cloth had been introduced from India in the 17th century and included chintz, a brightly-printed, fine material that caused a stir in the higher echelons of our society. Under protest from the silk and woollen industries, Parliament prohibited the import of this cloth, a move that, as usual, merely made it more desirable! It was a natural step to start importing raw cotton and to weave the cotton cloth here in England. Early cotton weavers used wooden hand blocks to print their cloth, not as good as the Indian chintz but its cheaper price created a wide demand. The wool and silk industries were not impressed and, in 1720, the import or wearing of any dyed or printed cotton, English or Indian, was made illegal. The loophole was that a mixed fabric of cotton and flax, called fustian, was not banned and the cotton industry turned to producing this. Eventually in 1774 the ban was lifted and the cotton industry took off. Partly due to the presence of the Liverpool docks, the embryo cotton

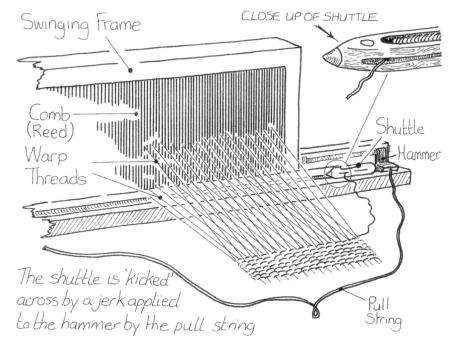

Swinging Frame

CLOSE UP OF SHUTTLE

Comb (Reed)

Warp Threads

Shuttle

Hammer

The shuttle is 'kicked' across by a jerk applied to the hammer by the pull string

Pull String

FIG 6.8: *The flying shuttle enabled the cloth to be made wider as the shuttle could be kicked further than a man could reach with the old hand stick.*

industry had started in Lancashire. The fact that this was a new material, unencumbered by years of tradition, and that it was confined to one geographical area allowed the mechanisation to take place at an incredible rate. Cotton is processed in a very similar way to wool; it is carded, teased out and spun into a twisted thread and then woven on a loom.

The first development was the flying shuttle, an improvement on the hand stick. The shuttle carries a bobbin wound with the weft thread and was kicked across the shed by a blow from a hammer which, in turn, was flicked by a cord held by the weaver. Invented by John Kay in 1733, initially for the wool industry, it enabled wider cloth to be woven, and faster too. So concerned were the weavers, fearing loss of work, that they attacked Kay's home, eventually forcing him to leave the country.

The next step was to mechanise the spinning wheel. The spinning jenny was invented by a humble weaver and carpenter from Blackburn, James Hargreaves, in 1764. It allowed for eight cotton threads to be drawn out on a moving frame and then spun and wound as the frame returned. The thread produced was weaker than traditional spinning and was only used for the weft thread. Workers, again fearful for their jobs, destroyed Hargreaves' home just four years later. As always, though, progress will out, and by the early 1780s some 20,000 jennies were in use in Lancashire.

FIG 6.9: *The spinning jenny. This replaced all three stages of the spinning wheel. The sliver of carded cotton was thinned by retracting the top frame (A), then twisted whilst the threads were held high by the bar (B) and finally wound onto the bobbins by slowly lowering the bar as the top frame moved forward.*

Produced in larger sizes and adapted for wool and flax, they were always powered by hand. Some even lasted into the 20th century.

Richard Arkwright was a barber and wig maker in Lancashire and was well aware of the growing cotton industry. In the late 1760s, he realised that the method of drawing raw cotton into a thread, at the time slow and labour intensive, could be improved. He produced his first machine to automate the spinning process in 1769. As a wig maker, Arkwright travelled extensively to arrange for the supply of hair (wigs used real hair in those days), including the Nottingham knitting area. This is where the seed of his idea may have been planted and John Kay, a Warrington clock maker (not the flying shuttle inventor), probably devised the mechanism.

His first working machine had four spindles and, with what was a massive leap of imagination, he realised that there was nothing to stop him making

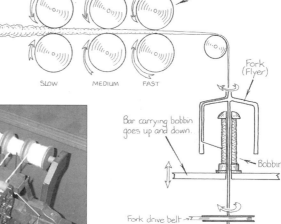

FIG 6.10: *Diagram showing the idea behind Arkwright's water frame. The rollers replaced the use of the fingers to tease out the raw sliver of wool or cotton.*

FIG 6.11: *The real thing – on show in the Museum of Science & Industry in Manchester. Note that with all machines the sliver of carded wool or cotton is much thinner than it comes from the first carding. The thicker roving has to be thinned and wound onto bobbins before it can be handled by either the spinning jenny or the water frame.*

FIG 6.12: *A 66-spindle mule, shown here fully retracted. The bar carrying the bobbins (lower row in picture) will move out across the floor on tracks, drawing out the sliver. Museum of Science & Industry, Manchester.*

FIG 6.13: *In the spinning mills dozens of frames were set out in great rows, all working in step. Here the bobbin frames have almost reached the end of their journey and will soon be returning to the left, bobbins madly spinning. Helmshore Mills Textile Museum.*

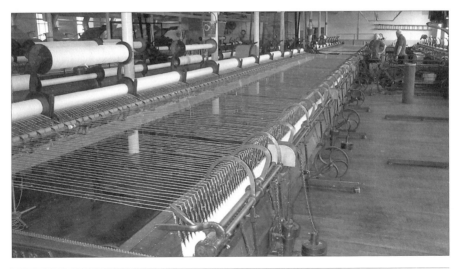

much bigger machines with up to 96 spindles. Borrowing money heavily, he opened the first factory mill near Cromford in 1771, using waterwheels to provide the power. He chose Derbyshire, incidentally, to be well away from Lancashire so as not to run the risk of angry workers breaking his machines. They still managed to burn down the first mill he did build in Lancashire some years later! It was claimed that just one unskilled man could now look after a 96-spindle machine. When Arkwright died in 1792, he left mills, a castle and a £500,000 fortune.

FIG 6.14: *First carding stage; all the carded material is drawn into a single roving.*

The next step was to combine the finer thread of the spinning jenny with the strength of the thread produced by the water frame. This was achieved by Samuel Crompton, in 1779, when he devised the mule. Basically, this is a fully mechanised spinning jenny but built much larger. In this machine, the already thinned out roving is drawn out as the bobbins move several feet across the floor. On the return the thread is twisted and wound onto the bobbins. Crompton didn't patent his idea and many manufacturers developed these machines, which grew to an enormous size and are quite alarming to see working. Not only did they produce a finer thread but, after a few years of refinement, they were able to draw threads down to the equivalent of 15 denier nylon.

FIG 6.15: *Second stage carding where the material is separated early on into several thinner slivers, which are wound either onto bobbins or as here onto long drums. It is these finer slivers that the water frames and mules use to make the thread. Both machines are from the excellent collection on display at the Helmshore Mills Textile Museum.*

FIG 6.16: *The finished loom, still only weaving plain cloth, with just one shuttle and a pair of heald frames lifting the warp threads. Museum of Science & Industry, Manchester.*

These are the machines that were kept clean of fluff and debris by very young children, who scrambled about on the floor quickly learning when to duck as the mule careered around above them. You will notice that the size of the slivers used in these later machines is small enough to be held on bobbins or drums. It had been found impossible to thin down the original thick roving to a single thread by machine in one go, so further carding stages had been introduced. This not only enabled the slivers to be made thinner to suit the machines, but also produced a yet more consistent mixture of fibres.

By 1785, Edmund Cartwright had produced the first waterwheel-driven loom in which all the manual actions were carried out mechanically. The shuttle was sent flying across the shed by a moving arm and a leather strap, travelling at around 60 m.p.h. The comb was now moved back and forth by another mechanism and the resultant cloth was wound steadily onto a revolving tube. The only task for the operator was to refresh the shuttles,

FIG 6.17: *Masson Mills near Cromford, built by Richard Arkwright in 1783 to produce thread. Originally powered by waterwheels fed by the river Derwent, which flows behind the mill, it was greatly extended as the years went by.*

which only carried a limited amount of thread and needed replacement every six or seven minutes, equivalent to just over twelve inches of cloth. Thus, one person, invariably a woman, could look after many machines. The original machines were far from perfect and development went on well into the 1820s before a truly reliable machine could be made.

Unlike cotton, woollen cloth from these early machines still needed a lot of hand finishing, which cost money. This, added to the enormous investment needed, meant that the mechanised mills didn't really become profitable until well into the 1830s. At this time,

there were still some 500,000 men producing cloth, working at hand looms, mostly in their homes. Given the now proven profitability and the arrival of steam engines to replace the waterwheels, mechanised mills multiplied and the home-based hand-loom industry started a steady decline.

Lancashire had become the centre for cotton work, partly because its damp climate suited the cotton threads and partly as it had plenty of water to drive the waterwheels. Mainly, though, it was Liverpool where the cotton, firstly from India and then from America, arrived. All these early mills used waterwheels for their power but as larger, reliable

FIG 6.18: *An example of a mill engine, which used cotton ropes running in a grooved flywheel to transmit power to other floors. This is one of many engines on display in the Museum of Science & Industry in Manchester.*

steam engines became available in the 1830s the mills slowly changed over. Just one 100 hp engine could drive 50,000 spindles! At the same time, in America, Eli Whitney had developed the cotton gin, which speeded up the separating of the cotton fibres from the seeds. An idea of the increase in production can be gained from the fact that American cotton exports rose 600-fold during this period.

Richard Arkwright had started the mass production of thread in factories and now the weaving followed – the dark satanic mills had arrived.

Like flax, cotton needed a high humidity whilst being worked on machines. In summer the floors of the mills were kept wet and in winter they were kept damp and cold; not the ideal conditions for working in!

Originally the power from massive waterwheels was transmitted via shafts and gears to all the floors in the mill. These overhead shafts then drove belts down to the machines. Later, steam engines did the same job and, later still, cotton ropes driven by an enormous grooved drum were used to transmit the power to the various floors and machines.

All the above has described making an even, flat cloth but it had long been realised that if the warp threads were

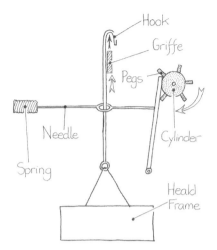

FIG 6.19: *The heald frame is lifted by the griffe, a bar of metal which is raised or lowered at the appropriate time. However, if the hook is moved over before the griffe rises then the griffe will not lift that particular hook or its heald frame. Which hook is moved out of the way is controlled by moving the needle that holds the hook. In the case shown – a simple cam system – the pattern is determined by rotating the cams. These mechanisms are mounted high above the loom in an assembly called a 'dobby'.*

FIG 6.20: *A cam 'dobby'. This uses wooden pegs fixed in a cylinder to convey an eight-position pattern.*

handled differently then textures and patterns could be achieved. If, instead of moving every other warp thread, one arranged for three sets of heald frames, one could now lift all the No 1 threads then pass the shuttle across, next all the No 2 threads and lastly all the No 3 threads. This gives a different texture to the cloth and by arranging for various combinations of the three groups, textures like the twill patterns can be produced. Typically, four heald frames

will produce a finish like a good quality tea towel, with five frames producing cloth like denim.

First developed in silk weaving where the threads are so fine that weft threads can miss several warp threads and not become weak, the idea was soon developed to enable different coloured weft threads to be interwoven, with the grouping of the warp threads becoming ever more complex. Originally, children were employed to pull the strings that determined which group of warp threads were lifted but, because they worked on exhausting ten-hour shifts, they became unreliable and made mistakes. One simple mistake could ruin a whole length of expensive silk, so something had to be done. The process cried out to be automated and that is what happened. Various

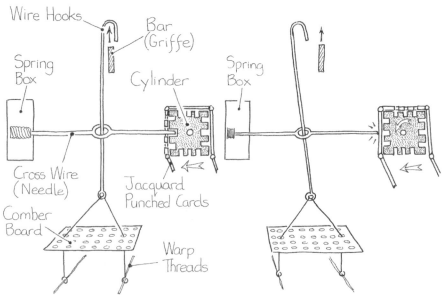

FIG 6.21: *In the Jacquard system the simple cams are replaced by the punched cards. The cards can carry a large number of holes and thus control many warp threads – so many in fact that the heald frame is abandoned and each hook lifts groups of individual warp threads. The cards, one for each pass of the weft thread, are strung out in a great loop rather like the music for a fairground organ.*

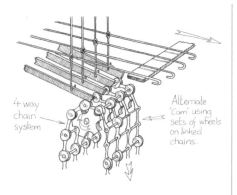

FIG 6.22: *Yet another variation – rather like the rotating cams but a chain system instead. Usually only 4 or 8 cams wide, the pattern can take many feet of chain before it repeats.*

mechanisms were designed that allowed elaborate patterns to be produced. The looms were adapted to have several shuttles as well, each one carrying a different coloured weft thread. They were laid in a frame that could be raised or lowered by the weaver pulling on yet another string to select which shuttle would be moved across the cloth next.

Using gears and cams to control the warp threads is fine if you are going to make a lot of cloth to the same pattern, but the silk industry in particular needed to be able to produce small runs of different designs. This led to the development of the Jacquard system in

FIG 6.23: *The Jacquard mechanism in its full glory. Each card carries 50 holes in 8 rows – that's 400 hole positions – which control 400 individual hooks, each of which lifts 8 warp threads. That's 3,200 warp threads! These looms are on show in the Masson Mills Working Textile Museum.*

which the pattern is stored on punched cards, which are then rotated until the whole pattern is achieved. The clever bit is how to lift the appropriate group of warp threads dependent on the holes punched in a card. Several mechanisms were designed, but the common principle is to have lightly sprung plungers that either pass through a hole on the card or are restrained by the absence of a hole. These plungers then control a mechanism that applies the necessary force to allow a group of threads to be raised. Thus, the cards themselves do not handle any high forces and last a long time. They are punched on a separate machine by a very skilled operator who follows a pre-drawn pattern. Finally, the cards are stitched together to form the whole sequence.

Dyeing

Dyes were obtained from vegetable matter such as saffron, turmeric and wood. The wood was reduced to chippings, which were ground to extract the dye. Different wood gave different colours. Later on, the range of colours was extended by using woods from overseas. South American woods were used for the yellows, pinks and reds whilst woods from New Zealand produced a golden brown. These dyes needed further help from chemicals called mordants, before they would adhere to the fabrics. The most important mordant was alum

FIG 6.24: *A horse-powered wood crushing gin at the Avoncroft Museum of Historic Buildings.*

produced from shale outcrops, mainly in Yorkshire. The processes involved in extracting these early chemicals represent the start of the chemical industry, which was to blossom in the 1850s with synthetic dyes leading the way.

Originally, the whole finished cloth would be dyed but very early on just the thread was dyed, enabling the multi-coloured patterns produced by the Jacquard looms to be made.

Dyeing was, in some ways, alien to the rest of the textile industry, having nothing to do with producing cloth. It thus developed as an independent industry, physically removed from the mills. Indeed, the mills often concentrated on just thread production

or just weaving, making the industry into a three-stage process.

From the early 1800s it had been realised that by mixing filaments from different grades of wool or mixing wool and cotton, one could produce a thread with different characteristics. As synthetic and polymer threads arrived in the late 1800s these too were mixed with wool and cotton, producing cloth we are familiar with today like the cotton/polyester mixes.

In many of the textile museums, you will see early spinning machines that combine fine threads together, either to achieve a thicker thread or to produce multi-coloured thread.

Even in the 1800s the dyeing works took the basic threads and coloured

FIG 6.25: *A teasel mill. The rotating drum has slots in it, into which are fixed teasels. These are carefully dried and shaped to produce row after row of hooks over which the cloth is drawn. This relatively rare example is in the Armley Mills Industrial Museum in Leeds.*

them as dictated by the fashion gurus of the day. Today the same system is used, with the dyeing industry setting up the next year's fashionable colours some eighteen months before the finished garments hit the shops. The same dyeing industry also treats the leathers and accessories to create a matching range of goods.

Most cloth is rolled, pressed or brushed after weaving. Wool, in particular, had the fluff raised by teasels. Initially these were hand held like hairbrushes; later they were mechanised. The pile created was then cut, firstly by hand held shears and, later, mown, like a lawn, by machines. Indeed the lawn mower came about after its inventor saw this process in a woollen mill. These finishing processes probably required more skill than the now fully mechanised thread and weaving stages.

Knitting

Knitting is, in effect a different way of weaving wool or silk. It too developed into a regional industry centred in the

FIG 6.26: *Two different types of knitting machine. On the left is a traditional home knitting machine; it is more complex than a loom and difficult to work. On the right is a stocking knitting machine, equally complex but easier to operate. Both examples are on display in the Nottingham Industrial Museum.*

East Midlands. The single thread is formed into a series of loops, held on a needle in hand knitting. The next row is simply another series of loops but these are drawn through the loops of the previous row. Started by the need for stockings, particularly for fashion-conscious men of the 15th century, knitting produces a much more elastic cloth than weaving. It is also relatively easy to shape the cloth by increasing or reducing the number of loops (stitches) in each row, a trick virtually impossible on a loom.

The home knitter worked for the local hosier, who not only supplied the yarn and collected the work but also rented the knitting frames. This rent was deducted from the knitter's earnings and was a source of unrest as it had to be paid regardless of whether there was any work or not. A typical large hosiery firm would operate home workers over an area of 20 or more miles. In 1844, a good worker could earn up to £37 a year when times were good.

Felt

Felt, a very old material like linen, can be made from a variety of natural fibres, including wool, but the best felts are

FIG 6.27: *Most knitting was concentrated in the East Midlands, but other areas also had small local industries. These knitters' cottages are in Tewkesbury and, though now converted to modern housing, the tell-tale wide windows give a clue to their original use. Similar large windows can be found in the cottages of the Lancashire and Yorkshire home weaving areas.*

made from animal hair, in particular, beaver pelts. The process follows the other natural fibres as far as the cleaning and carding goes but then takes a completely different route. The loose fibres are laid together to form a thin layer with no sense of direction to the fibres. In the machine-made version, this is done by putting the fibres onto a shaped sieve from which air is being drawn out. Rather like a filter in a vacuum cleaner, it produces a layer of interwoven fibres.

This first 'cloth' is frail and will fall apart if not handled carefully. The next stage involves pressing the cloth in boiling water, which binds the fibres together – a risky and dangerous job.

The effect was not understood until modern microscopes revealed what was going on: the fibres are, in fact, covered in minute hooks (super Velcro) and the hot water treatment makes the hooks curl tighter; the pressing simply allows the hooks of adjacent fibres to interlock. This is followed by various pressing, heating and dyeing processes to produce the finished felt.

Felt has a very clever trick up its sleeve involving shellac varnish. Used in making hats in particular, when shellac is added to felt it collects in the centre, leaving the surfaces apparently unaltered. Once dry, the shellac stiffens the felt and adds a degree of waterproofing.

FIG 6.28: *Part of the felt making process shown in detail in the Hat Works in Stockport. The blown, mixed fibres are drawn into this machine at the top and, using an air pump, the fibres are sucked onto the perforated cone (white in the centre of the window). Soon an even layer of fibres builds up over the cone.*

SECTION III

THE
SUPPORTING
CAST

CHAPTER 7

Agriculture

I have looked in some detail at four major groups of industrial activity that are still well represented in our industrial museums. However, there were few, if any, activities that were not touched by the Industrial Revolution.

In the next five chapters I want to look briefly at just five more industries, which provided materials or services to the main industrial expansion. Each made use of the latest iron and steam engine developments and in their more efficient form returned the favour by serving the iron and engine industries all the better.

Throughout our early history, agriculture was always the biggest employer, but, during the 18th century, it felt the touch of science, with a more informed understanding of breeding livestock and of selecting the best seed strains. There is a lovely chicken and egg dilemma relating to this period. Some believe that the arrival of better farming methods created thousands of out-of-work farm workers, who left the countryside to become the labour force for the rapidly expanding industrial factories. Others believe that the better conditions of factory work – rural farm life was pretty dreadful – attracted the workers away from the farms, driving the need

FIG 7.1: *Iron was now relatively cheap and could be easily applied to all manner of tools. The humble horse-drawn plough is a good example, being strong and able to cut through roots and stony ground with ease.*

to improve farming methods to cope with the reduced workforce. Farming, nevertheless, pressed on with more efficient machines, the Enclosure Acts and improved husbandry.

Early in the 1700s, Viscount Townshend promoted a new system of crop rotation. Traditionally the cycle was two years of crops, followed by one year left fallow. He suggested a four-year cycle: typically wheat, clover, barley or oats and, lastly, turnips. The clover put nitrogen back into the soil and supported cattle or sheep which also added fertiliser. The turnips provided nutrients for the soil and then became a winter feed for the animals, which otherwise were slaughtered each autumn. This seemingly casual side effect changed the keeping of cattle completely – fresh meat was now available all year round, as was milk.

From around 1780, with a steadily growing population, landowners now looked on their estates as a source of profit, and farming moved from a basic necessity to a professionally run business. The increased availability of cheap, locally worked iron improved the tools, seed drills and ploughs.

By the early 1800s, movable steam engines had arrived, allowing all manner of farming processes to be mechanised. In addition to the familiar ploughing and threshing, less obvious activities benefited: uprooting trees and hedges to make bigger fields, cutting drainage trenches and laying pipes to prevent the fields becoming boggy, even making the drainage pipes on site. By the 1860s, farming was a stable and entrenched industry but it was about to be awoken by two events. America and

FIG 7.2: *Though these are machines from the early 20th century, scenes like this would have been common throughout the second half of the 19th century.*

Canada were now producing vast crops of wheat and corn (often promoted by the new railroads) and large steam-driven ships were available to transport the grain to Europe. The second event was the invention of refrigeration. Ships could now move quantities of chilled meat from Australia, New Zealand and Argentina. All this new food arrived in our docks at a fraction of the cost of the home-produced version.

One aspect of farming that is very well represented in our museums is flour production. Though the principles are ancient, grinding corn in waterwheel-driven mills and windmills reached a golden age during the Industrial

FIG 7.3: A post mill in which the entire working part was turned to face the wind. The brick base merely acts as protection for the post and gives added storage. Avoncroft Museum of Historic Buildings.

Revolution. Like many early machines these are basically simple and fairly obvious processes, though this simplicity hides a wealth of cunning and clever knowledge.

We have examined the various waterwheel arrangements already so a brief look at windmills would be appropriate.

Windmills work by keeping their sails facing into the wind but this means that the sails must be turned as the wind changes. The early post mills did this by turning almost the entire building. The sails were literally just that, wooden frames with canvas stretched over them. The first sails were symmetrical about the stock but by the 17th century a more aerodynamic sail had been devised, known as the common sail.

Windmills had steadily grown in size during the centuries up to 1700 but as demand grew and metalwork skills improved we see improvements in the basic structures.

The early post mills had largely given way to tower and smock mills, in which only the sails and first part of the gearing turned to face the wind. The rest of the mill and all the grinding machines were stationary within the main part of the building. This allowed a more substantial construction to be used in the mill tower, which could now carry the ever-increasing weight of bigger sails. Smock mills were constructed in timber; they were often six sided and vaguely resembled a man wearing a smock. Tower mills were constructed of stone or brick.

The job of keeping the sails facing the

wind, originally done by hand, was solved in the 1700s by having a second small windwheel fixed at right angles to the main sail and used to drive gears which turned the whole assembly around. This second windwheel – the fantail – would thus drive until it lost all wind, which occurred when its sails were at right angles to the wind direction. Because the fantail sails were at a right angle to the main sails this point was exactly where the main sails needed to be in order to face straight into the wind.

In early mills, the miller controlled the speed of the sails by altering the sail area. This was done by stopping each sail in turn and manually altering the amount of cloth over the sail frame. During the 1700s, changes were made to the sails, the cloth being replaced by a system of adjustable slats, rather like a venetian blind. These allowed gusts of wind to pass through the sails without causing damage and, following more development, it was possible to adjust the slats from the ground so the miller now had much better control of the speed than ever before. These improvements were typical of the effect the Industrial Revolution had on life. The widespread availability of good metalwork allowed improvements to modest, everyday equipment used in agriculture.

The task of utilising the rotating energy was similar to the process of the waterwheel. The horizontal shaft that carried the sails had the same strength problems as the waterwheel and its motion was transmitted in the same way; this time going down the mill

FIG 7.4: *The fantail turns a shaft that enters the top of the mill, where it drives a gear wheel that engages in a toothed rack laid around the top of the tower. Any rotation of the fantail thus turns the entire cap around.*

rather than up. The pit wheel now becomes the brake wheel but all the other gear names remain as in waterwheels. The name 'brake wheel' also highlights a basic difference between waterwheels and windmills. In the former, one could simply turn the water supply on and off but one couldn't do that with the wind. Imagine the early post mill: the miller has opened the sail material on the first of the four sails and off goes the windmill! He has to be able to hold the sails under control in order to set them and to stop the mill when necessary, hence a brake that can be applied to the sail shaft. It usually took the form of a band around the outer rim

FIG 7.5: *A very early French roller mill using porcelain rollers on display in Cauldwell's Mill, Rowsley, Matlock.*

of the brake wheel, which could be tightened to slow the wheel down.

Just as the waterwheel survived long into the 19th century so did windmills. Again, they were simple to build and cheap to operate, and there wasn't any better way, provided that the process they powered could wait during a period of low wind.

Just as the products of the revolution had aided cheap foodstuffs to arrive from abroad so, too, was the flour grinding operation changed, heralding the demise of both the watermill and windmill. In the 1860, a new way to grind flour had been developed in central Europe, the roller mill. Not only was it able to produce great quantities but it better suited the harder American grain. Massive roller mills were built, usually near rivers or ports so that the grain ships could dock alongside.

The mechanisation of agriculture is well displayed at the outdoor traction engine shows. You can see ploughing, threshing and tree sawing, plus dozens of steam engines of all sizes, but with everything biased toward farming and rural workshop usage. The magazine *Old Glory* gives full details of these shows. Many local museums also have collections of early farm machinery on display.

CHAPTER 8

Coal

The very earliest mining in Britain involved shallow workings for flint. By the Bronze Age, lead, tin and copper were being mined and, possibly, small quantities of coal. The Saxons and Danes, however, appeared to have no interest in coal and there is no mention of it in the Domesday Book. By the time of the Magna Carta, coal was being gathered from outcrops around the Tyne and Wear rivers. Its use in domestic heating started only very slowly due to the noxious fumes and poor ventilation. The glass and lead industries had been forced into using coal during the 17th century but it was not until the development of coke for the iron industry that demand really grew. It was this same iron industry that enabled the making of better pumps so that mines could go deeper, along with better machines to cut the coal and get it to the surface.

Many coal seams are, or rather were, exposed at the surface. Thus, the early small quantities were obtained with little digging at all. Later, bell-shaped pits were dug down some 20 to 30 ft to

FIG 8.1: *Early mining used horse gins to move both the men and the coal up and down the mine shafts. Some early attempts at removing water also used horse gins. This example is at the Bersham Heritage Centre near Wrexham.*

FIG 8.2: *This reconstructed small mine is in the Blists Hill Museum at Ironbridge, complete with the small coal wagons, which were loaded down in the mine and sent up to the surface thus avoiding unloading the coal within the mine itself.*

FIG 8.3: *This larger mine has been constructed in the North of England Open Air Museum at Beamish. Like the Black Country site, Beamish was also a heavy coal mining area and also gives visitors a chance to experience going underground. The large raised 'sheds' are where the coal was graded before being dropped into railway wagons for transportation.*

reach shallow coal seams. Drift mines were dug by simply following the seam of coal into a hillside. Because they were usually worked by just a few men, they tended to be small and local. In the Forest of Dean, drift mining even continued into the 20th century.

By the 1600s, attempts to get coal from deeper seams were hindered by problems of ventilation and water. In 1606, boring was developed to help locate the coal before the expensive task of sinking shafts was undertaken. Early ventilation was achieved by having two shafts and lighting a fire beneath one of them. The hot air rose up this upcast shaft and, in turn, drew fresh air down the other, downcast, shaft. A system of doors, operated by children, was used to direct the fresh air around the workings. Mechanical air pumps were developed in the early 1830s and were used in all the larger mines from then on. Despite this, explosions caused by a build-up of methane gas and fine coal dust continued and haunted the mining areas for years.

Removing water was the problem that gave birth to the steam engine, as we have seen earlier. Another 72 years were to pass before a steam engine was trusted with winding, giving the somewhat odd situation of a steam engine pumping water whilst a horse still plodded around the gin to lift coal and men up and down the mine shaft.

Like all industries during the Industrial Revolution period, mining

FIG 8.4: *Typical air pump used to ventilate a small local coal mine. This is an example of the Capell fan from the late 1800s; very efficient, it could move 60,000 cubic feet of air per minute. The fan was driven by a donkey engine housed in the corrugated shed to the right. Part of the Black Country Living Museum's mining exhibits.*

took advantage of every advance in engines and materials although, alas, only if it profited the owners. The coal mining industry must represent one of the worst exploitations of men, women and children ever to have taken place in Britain.

Coal mining reached its peak around 1913 and some idea of the vast quantities involved can be gained from the output of just one area. The Great Northern Coalfield in Durham employed nearly a quarter of a million men and boys and produced over one million tons of coal per week from over 400 pits.

The waste products from making coke included tar, coal gas and the first chemicals. Coal gas was quickly taken up for lighting and cooking, with every town or city having its own gasworks by the 1850s. All this coal, initially moved by canal, became the main goods traffic of the new railways for over 125 years. Its final use was in generating electricity which, like gas, was a local industry until the concept of the national grid made today's massive power stations feasible.

Many museums feature coal mining, including the chance to go underground and absorb the dreadful atmosphere and working conditions. Beware – some sites are still dusty so don't visit in your Sunday best!

FIG 8.5: *Not coal but the transhipment point for minerals mined in Devon. Lead, tin, magnesium and copper all featured at one time here in Morwellham.*

Canals and Railways

FIG 9.1: *Pre Industrial Revolution heavy transport! Modern-day sailing ships in the old china clay harbour at Charlestown in Cornwall help to give an idea of a bygone age.*

It is very difficult to imagine the world of the 1750s. Everywhere, industrial ideas were awakening but still the only way to transport heavy goods was by river or sea. Horse-drawn carts and the pack horse were still the only inland transport available. Needing mainly wood, stone and clay – all local products – the first canal works predate the revolution by some 100 years but the need to move coal was the driving force that started the main canal system in the 1770s. By 1835, over 2,500 miles of inland waterways had been built and conveyed coal, steel and food.

Virtually nothing is left of the early canal buildings and boats, mainly because, like so many industrial activities, they were constantly updated and improved. But we still have much of the canal system and plenty of working boats which, though rarely over 100 years old, still convey the atmosphere of the working canal system.

Horse-drawn tramways had been used for many years. They were mainly associated with quarries and indeed many were built to bring minerals to the canal network for onward carriage. The jump to railways, as we think of them, was one of those timely meetings of need and means. Coal was the need, iron and steam engines were the means. Originally, the rails were made of wood pinned into stone blocks, a method which kept the path between

FIG 9.2: *Early engravings, such as this rather romantic example from 1873, provide the best idea of very early canal and river boat work, though before the 1840s it was an all male preserve.*

FIG 9.3: *The canal scene today, showing a restored working boat at the Ellesmere Boat Museum.*

the rails clear for the horses. By the 1730s, iron wheels had appeared and the wooden rails were topped with iron plates to reduce the wear and tear. The wheels were still like cart wheels and were kept in place by the flanges on the sides of the rails. Within a few years, cast iron flanged rails were made, so-called 'plateways', some of which carried on into the 20th century. Edge rails, where the flange is on the wheel (like modern railways) were tried early on but the L-shaped flanged rails were claimed to be stronger and had the added advantage that the trucks could run from the railway onto flat surfaces, though it is doubtful if this was ever done.

Most lines at this time were built to take wagons to wharfs beside rivers and canals for onward shipment, though one line, the Surrey Iron Railway, built in 1803 from Wandsworth to Croydon, was opened to carry passengers rather

FIG 9.4: *Two examples of cast iron flanged rail.*

FIG 9.5: *An example of an early engine from the collection at the North of England Open Air Museum, Beamish. It was built for the Hetton colliery in 1851, though based on a much earlier design. This engine is no longer working – the boiler is made from cast iron plates and can't be made safe enough to use – but bone-shaking rides behind other replica early engines are still run.*

than minerals. By the 1820s, several of these horse-drawn passenger lines had opened and the scene was set for the steam locomotive to blossom. Flanged rails were fine for slow-moving traffic but, as speeds increased, the edge rail won the day. The shape of the rail top and the profile of the wheels provided an automatic centring effect. The rails were now simply weight bearing and were made of rolled wrought iron until the arrival of mass-produced steel in

FIG 9.6: *Today the preserved railway movement provides a glimpse of late Victorian travel, although this engine, on the Severn Valley Railway at Bewdley, is 1930s' vintage.*

1856. This solved the speed and weight limitations of iron, and so track and engines leapt ahead, quickly outgrowing the canal system. Eventually, some 23,000 miles of track carried virtually everything that needed moving for nearly a hundred years until the motor lorry and the diesel engine arrived.

Though much of the inventing had been done earlier, it is this 1830 to 1850 period that saw the real expansion of industry. Production methods were now established and machines were trouble-free and reliable. The railways captured this confidence completely, with bridges, tunnels and stations of immense size and daring, forming the arteries of the nation.

Both the canal and railway heritage scenes are well covered by magazines, which give details of sites and events.

FIG 9.7: *The delightful setting for the National Waterways Museum in Gloucester. The docks are surrounded by these superb warehouses, for which new uses are slowly being found.*

CHAPTER 10

Factories

The concept of making a product using the same materials, jigs or machines over and over again defines the factory. The product cost is lower than the equivalent item made in small quantities by local craftsmen. It does, however, require investment to set up and thus a degree of judgement in those being asked to back the venture. To illustrate this, I want to describe two enterprises unrelated to the previously discussed industries, both of which paved the way for the end of the craftsman. At the start of the 19th century, Marc Brunel (Isambard's father) had come across the manufacture of pulley blocks in the naval dockyards in Portsmouth. Each warship used approximately 2,000 blocks to control the sails and rigging, as well as moving the guns and other heavy loads. Every block was hand made and Brunel felt that it must be possible to improve this slow process. He knew Henry Maudslay who was a most ingenious man and

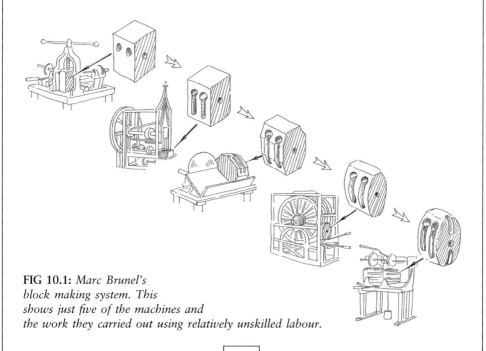

FIG 10.1: *Marc Brunel's block making system. This shows just five of the machines and the work they carried out using relatively unskilled labour.*

was to become the leading producer of machines in the country. Between them they worked away for some six years and eventually produced a set of 44 machines, each designed to perform one stage of the pulley block's manufacture. The effect was startling: ten relatively unskilled men could now make 130,000 blocks per year. Though, to us, a perfectly obvious way to produce something, it was a revolution in 1806. In one of those strange ways that England has of inventing something but then failing to exploit it, the principle of the factory production line, so ably put together by Brunel in Portsmouth, was not taken up in England and next appears in America.

The second example is Josiah Wedgwood's pottery works at Etruria in Stoke-on-Trent, where the idea of a single craftsman producing an entire product was laid to rest. In 1769, just ten years after he had set up on his own account, Wedgwood was at the peak of his career. Here the actual process was not altered but instead each worker did just one part of it. They now required a narrower field of knowledge and the work became more repetitive and did not offer the satisfaction of completing the object being made. More important to the factory owner, however, was that the workers only needed the skills associated with their particular task not the whole process. In effect, this meant the end of the craftsman.

The adoption of the factory system necessitated bringing all the workers together close to the factory, hence the mass housing that typified the 1800s. The lot of the factory worker varied, some factory owners being most benevolent whilst others were tight-fisted.

Many of the larger museums have housing, shops and works representing, at least, the late Victorian era, which help convey the feel of these early factory living areas.

FIG 10.2: *Wedgwood's factory at Etruria in Stoke-on-Trent, facing onto the Trent and Mersey Canal, which he had actively supported. Not only could his materials now arrive by boat but his growing export market could be served via Liverpool. Breakages by road transport were horrific but the boats changed that for good.*

CHAPTER 11

Buildings

A s the population grew steadily through the 1700s and into the 1800s, the demand for buildings and the materials to construct them increased. Stone had always been carried great distances where the cost of transport could be justified; stone from Rutland to Windsor Castle, or Purbeck stone to as far away as Durham Cathedral. The advent of better transport, firstly the canals and then railways, allowed geographically isolated materials like stone and slate to be moved cheaply to all the developing areas. For most of the country, though, bricks were still the building material of choice, being cheap and locally produced.

Bricks are a very old building material going back thousands of years. Clay was dug up in the autumn and left for the winter rains and frosts to break it up. In spring it was wetted and stones were removed, and then the clay was placed in wooden moulds and left to dry. Originally the 'green' bricks,

FIG 11.1: *Local brickworks moulded their name into the bricks and this now gives us some idea of just how widespread brickworks were. This collection is in the Blists Hill Museum, Ironbridge.*

FIG 11.2: *Typical local brickworks, part of the Blists Hill Museum, Ironbridge, where brick making is still demonstrated.*

still rather soft, were set out to dry in the sunshine. By the 15th century, this drying was being done in kilns using an underfloor fire to provide the heat, producing a much stronger and fairly waterproof brick. The brick making industry grew steadily, despite the government placing a tax on bricks in 1784. This tax was eventually withdrawn in 1850, by which time the output had reached 1,800 million bricks a year. Mechanisation was slowly

FIG 11.3: *Victorian cobbled street. Britain still has countless miles of sturdy brick-built houses. These form part of the Black Country Living Museum.*

introduced, firstly for the working of the clay and then the moulding. Both underfloor heating and conventional kilns were used until, in 1858, a continuous kiln was invented by a German engineer, Friedrich Hoffman.

Roof tiles were made in a similar way and this side of the industry expanded into making the decorative glazed tiles so beloved of the Victorian era. Slowly, though, unseen and often unheralded, piped water and sewage removal arrived. The early Roman pipes had been made from wood but clay and then iron pipes took over. Larger sewers were built of brick and, aided by the pipes and engines of the iron and steam industries, modern sanitation was born.

The other familiar construction component is glass, which has been made since 4,000 BC. By the time of the Industrial Revolution, hand blown glass was common, used for bottles, jars and crown window glass. Crown glass is made by allowing a blown globe of glass to collapse, under rotation, into a flat disc. The centre, where the glass is held, forms the crown. After polishing in a flame, the glass is cooled and cut up, the best glass being from the outer flat areas. By the 1830s, the cylinder method had been developed. In this process the glass is blown into a long bottle shape, sometimes as large as 20 inches (0.5 m) diameter by 70 inches (1.75 m) long. The glass is cooled, the ends cut off and a slit made lengthwise down the cylinder. It is then reheated and gently unrolled into a flat sheet. Cast plate glass was produced in England from around 1775 and though it formed the largest and best sheets it was expensive.

In parallel with all this building, the

FIG 11.4: *Plain looking but historically important. The smaller red brick mill building is Strutt's fireproof mill, built with iron frames and brick floors in 1804. It replaced the original building, which, like so many early mills, had burnt down. The vast extension to the left (North Mill, Belper) dates from 1912.*

road system improved, using drainage channels and hard surfaces supported on proper foundations, just as the Romans had done 2,000 years before. Tarmac and other industrial products arrived to give a more weatherproof surface. In the industrial sector, however, the arrival of iron produced some remarkable changes, with bridges being the most visually obvious, firstly for canals, then for roads and lastly for the railways. Structural ironwork in factories, originally used to attain a degree of fireproofing, was followed by iron frameworks, enabling taller buildings to be built.

Without doubt the most fitting finale to the Industrial Revolution era was the Crystal Palace of 1851. It showed just how much progress had been made, not just by the fact that it was built, but in the manner and speed. A desperate committee who, with less than a year to go, had already rejected some 240 possible designs, seized on Joseph Paxton's idea of a massive conservatory. The sheer size is amazing even to us today: over 600 yards (560 m) long, 135 yards (124 m) wide, 33 yards (30 m) high and involving some 3,500 tons of iron and 300,000 panes of glass. The secret lay in the repetition of the cast iron shapes and the identical glass panes. Nevertheless, to provide the materials and construct the building in less than ten months was incredible. It housed over 100,000 items from around the world. Intended as a flagship for British industry, it also sent a chill down the spines of the captains of industry as they saw just how much overseas progress (by the Americans, in particular) had been made. It was dismantled after a year, its original job done, and re-erected and extended in the part of London that still bears its name. Alas, it burnt to the ground in 1936, a sad end for a symbol of one of the greatest periods of English history.

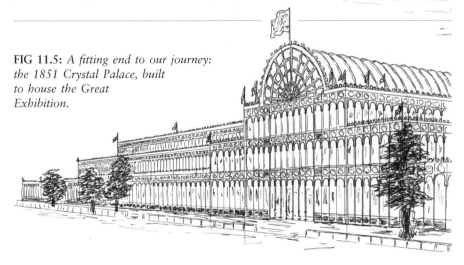

FIG 11.5: *A fitting end to our journey: the 1851 Crystal Palace, built to house the Great Exhibition.*

SECTION IV

REFERENCE

Museums and Sites to Visit

Possibly the most dramatic entrance to any industrial museum. You actually drive through this magnificent drop forge steam hammer, called 'Tiny Tim'. Built in 1883 it has a height of 35 ft and weighs in at a mere 90 tons.

Whilst there are some industrial artefacts that can be seen in the open, the vast majority are housed in museums. Entry to some of the larger national museums is now free but many are run by trusts or charities, which make a charge for entry.

When searching for museums, a good place to start is your local tourist information office or library. Here you can find leaflets on the local sites and often on larger ones elsewhere in the country. Several museums also have websites. Don't forget your local town museum; many provide excellent displays, often featuring the history of the local industries, and usually have leaflets for other similar sites in the same area.

Both the National Trust and English Heritage own industrial sites:

National Trust (NT):   Telephone: 0870 458 4000
Website: www.nationaltrust.org.uk

English Heritage (EH):   Telephone: 0870 333 1181
Website: www.english-heritage.org.uk

If all this searching sounds a bit like hard work, then I can recommend a book by Anthony Burton called *The Daily Telegraph Guide to Britain's Working Past*, which is probably the best catalogue of sites ever put together.

There are over 500 industrial sites and museums in the British Isles so the list given below is only a small selection. It includes (shown in italics) those sites that are featured in the book and hopefully will mention a site or two within your own area.

━━◆━━

London and South East

British Engineerium, Neville Road, Hove, Sussex
www.britishengineerium.com   Telephone: 01273 554070

Chart Gunpowder Mills, Faversham, Kent   Telephone: 01795 534542

Crabble Watermill, Dover, Kent   Telephone: 01304 823292

Kew Bridge Steam Museum, Green Dragon Lane, Brentford, London
www.kbsm.org   Telephone: 020 8568 4757

Kingsbury Watermill/Museum, St Albans, Hertfordshire Telephone: 01727 853502

Mill Green Mill, Hatfield, Hertfordshire: Working mill/museum
Telephone: 01707 271362

Science Museum, South Kensington, London
www.nmsi.ac.uk   Telephone: 020 7942 4000

Union Windmill, Cranbrook, Kent: Tallest in country   Telephone: 01580 712984

Weald & Downland Open Air Museum, Nr Chichester, Sussex
www.wealddown.co.uk   Telephone: 01243 811363

The South and South West

Burcott Watermill (NT), Dorset   Telephone: 01749 673118

Calbourne Watermill, Isle of Wight: Uses rollers   Telephone: 01983 531227

City Watermill (NT), Winchester, Hampshire   Telephone: 01962 870057

Crofton Pumping Station, Crofton, Wiltshire: England's oldest working beam engine
www.katrust.org   Telephone: 01672 870300

Coldharbour Woollen Mill, Uffculme, Devon: Worsted cloth
Telephone: 01884 840960

Cornish Mines & Engines, Trevithick Road, Pool, Cornwall
Telephone: 01209 315027

Dunster Watermill (NT), Dorset: Produces flour   Telephone: 01643 821759

Eling Tide Mill, Totton, Hampshire   Telephone: 01703 869575

Finch Foundry, Sticklepath, Nr Okehampton, Devon   Telephone: 01837 840046

Industrial Museum, Princes Wharf, City Docks, Bristol
www.bristol-city.gov.uk/museums   Telephone: 0117 9251470

Hollycombe Steam Collection, Liphook, Hampshire   Telephone: 01428 724900

Hopewell Colliery Museum, Coleford, Gloucestershire   Telephone: 01594 810706

Melinsey Waterwheel, Veryan, Cornwall: Museum/Crafts Telephone: 01872 501371

Morwellham Quay, Nr Tavistock, Devon
www.morwellham-quay.co.uk   Telephone: 01822 832766

Museum of Bath at Work, Julian Road, Bath, Somerset
www.bath-at-work.org.uk   Telephone: 01225 318348

National Waterways Museum, Gloucester Docks, Gloucester
Telephone: 01452 318054

Newcomen Engine, Dartmouth, Devon   Telephone: 01803 834224

Otterton Watermill, Devon: Grinds flour Telephone: 01395 568521

Westonzoyland Pumping Station, Westonzoyland, Somerset
Telephone: 01823 275795

Wheal Martyn China Clay Museum, St Austell, Cornwall
www.wheal-martyn.com Telephone: 01726 850362

East Anglia and East Midlands

Alford Windmill, Alford, Lincolnshire: Working 5-sailed tower mill
Telephone: 01507 462136

Bressingham Steam Museum, Norfolk Telephone: 01379 688585

Denver Windmill, Downham Market, Norfolk Telephone: 01366 384009

Forncett St Mary Steam Museum, Norfolk Telephone: 01508 488277

Gunton Park, Norfolk: Waterwheel-driven sawmill Telephone: 01603 222705

Houghton Watermill (NT), Cambridgeshire Telephone: 01480 301494

Long Shop Steam Museum, Main Street, Leiston, Suffolk
Telephone: 01728 832189

Mount Pleasant Windmill, Kirton, Lincolnshire Telephone: 01652 640177

Museum of East Anglian Life, Stowmarket, Suffolk Telephone: 01449 612229

Museum of Technology, Cheddlars Lane, Cambridge Telephone: 01223 368650

Pakenham Waterwheel & Windmill, Suffolk Telephone: 01359 230277

Pinchbeck Marsh Engine, Lincolnshire Telephone: 01775 725468

Strumpshaw Old Hall Steam Museum, Strumpshaw, Norfolk
Telephone: 01603 713392

Woodbridge Tide Mill, Suffolk Telephone: 01473 626618

Central, West and North Midlands

Abbey Pumping Station, Corporation Road, Leicester Telephone: 0116 2995111

Avoncroft Museum of Historic Buildings, Stoke Heath, Bromsgrove, Worcestershire
www.avoncroft.org.uk Telephone: 01527 831363

Black Country Living Museum, Tipton Road, Dudley, West Midlands
www.bclm.co.uk Telephone: 0121 5579643

Blists Hill: Part of the Ironbridge Gorge Trust sites

Boat Museum, South Pier Road, Ellesmere Port, Cheshire Telephone: 0151 3555017

Brindley Mill, Leek, Staffordshire Telephone: 01538 483741

Broomy Hill Waterworks, Hereford Telephone: 01432 344062

Calverton Folk Museum, Calverton, Nottinghamshire Telephone: 0115 9654843

Canal Museum, The, Stoke Bruerne, Towcester, Northamptonshire
www.thewaterwaystrust.co.uk Telephone: 01604 862229

Cauldwell's Mill, Rowsley, Nr Matlock, Derby Telephone: 01629 734374

Cheddleton Flint Mill, Leek, Staffordshire Telephone: 01782 502907

Claymills Pumping Station, Stretton, Burton upon Trent, Staffordshire
Telephone: 01283 509292

Coalbrookdale Museum of Iron: Part of the Ironbridge Gorge Trust sites

Cotswold Woollen Weavers, Filkins, Oxfordshire Telephone: 01367 860491

Daniels Mill, Eardington, Nr Bewdley, Shropshire Telephone: 01746 762753

Dean Heritage Museum, Upper Soudley, Gloucestershire Telephone: 01594 822170

Forge Mill Needle Museum, Redditch, Worcestershire Telephone: 01527 62509

Greens Mill, Nottingham Telephone: 0115 9156878

Hat Works, The, Stockport: Felt manufacture Telephone: 0161 3557770

Industrial Museum, The Silk Mill, Silk Mill Lane, Derby
www.derby.gov.uk/museums Telephone: 01332 255308

Ironbridge Gorge Trust (features 10 separate museums), Telford, Shropshire
www.ironbridge.org.uk Telephone: 01952 432166

Masson Mills Working Textile Museum, Matlock Bath, Derbyshire
www.massonmills.co.uk Telephone: 01629 581001

Middleton Top Engine House, Middleton by Winksworth, Derbyshire
Telephone: 01629 823204

Moira Furnace, Moira, Leicestershire Telephone: 01283 224667

Museum of Lace, Nottingham Telephone: 0115 9897365

Nether Alderley (NT), Wilmslow, Cheshire: Watermill Telephone: 01625 523012

North Mill, Belper, Derbyshire Telephone: 01773 880474

Nottingham Industrial Museum, Wollaton Park, Nottingham
Telephone: 0115 9153190

Papplewick Pumping Station, Ravenshead, Nottinghamshire
Telephone: 0115 9632938

Peak District Mining Museum, Matlock Bath, Derby
www.peakmines.co.uk   Telephone: 01629 583834

Quarry Bank (NT), Styal, Wilmslow
www.quarrybankmill.org.uk   Telephone: 01625 527468

Sarehole Mill, Hall Green, Birmingham   Telephone: 0121 3034698

Shore Road Pumping Station, Birkenhead, Cheshire   Telephone: 0151 6501182

Silk Museum, Park Lane, Macclesfield, Cheshire
www.silk-macclesfield.org   Telephone: 01625 613210

Snibston Discovery Park, Coalville, Leicestershire   Telephone: 01530 510851

Stretton Waterwheel, Nr Farndon, Cheshire   Telephone: 01606 41331

Thinktank, Millennium Point, Curzon Street, Birmingham, West Midlands
www.thinktank.ac   Telephone: 0121 3031655

Wellesbourne Watermill, Warwickshire   Telephone: 01789 470237

The North

Abbeydale Industrial Hamlet, Sheffield
www.simt.co.uk   Telephone: 0114 2367731

Armley Mills, Leeds Industrial Museum, Canal Road, Leeds
www.leeds.gov.uk/armleymills   Telephone: 0133 2637861

Bancroft Mill Engine, Gillians Lane, Barnoldswick, Lancashire
Telephone: 01282 813751

Bradford Industrial Museum, Moorside Mill, Eccleshill, Bradford
www.bradford.gov.uk   Telephone: 01274 631756

Colliery Museum, Astley Green, Lancashire   Telephone: 01942 828121

Colne Valley Museum, Golcar, Yorkshire   Telephone: 01484 659762

Darlington Railway Centre & Museum, Durham   Telephone: 01325 460532

Derwentcote Steel Furnace (EH), Hamsterley, Durham   Telephone: 01207 562573

Discovery Museum, Blandford Square, Newcastle upon Tyne
Telephone: 0191 2326789

Ellenroad Engine House, Elizabethan Way, Milnrow, Lancashire
Telephone: 01706 481952

Elsecar Heritage Centre, Elsecar, Yorkshire   Telephone: 01226 740203

Eskdale Watermill, Boot, Cumbria   Telephone: 019467 23335

Florence Mine, Egremont, Nr Whitehaven, Cumbria   Telephone: 01946 820683

Haig Colliery, Kells, Whitehaven, Cumbria   Telephone: 01946 599949

Heatherslaw Watermill, Ford, Northumberland   Telephone: 01890 820338

Helmshore Mills Textile Museum, Holcombe Road, Rossendale, Lancashire
www.lancsmuseums.gov.uk   Telephone: 01706 226459

Kelham Island Museum, Sheffield, Yorkshire: Headquarters of the Sheffield
Industrial Museums Trust; features steel making
www.simt.co.uk   Telephone: 0114 2367731

Lytham St Annes Windmill Museum, Cumbria   Telephone: 01253 794879

Magna Science Adventure Centre, Templeborough, Rotherham, Yorkshire
www.magnatrust.org.uk   Telephone: 01709 720002

Muncaster Watermill, Ravenglass, Cumbria   Telephone: 01229 717232

Museum of Science & Industry, Liverpool Road, Castlefield, Manchester
www.msim.org.uk   Telephone: 0161 8321380

National Coal Mining Museum, Overton, Yorkshire   Telephone: 01924 848806

National Railway Museum, York   Telephone: 01904 621261

North of England Open Air Museum, Beamish, Durham
www.beamish.org.uk   Telephone: 01207 231811

Ryhope Pumping Station, Sunderland, Tyne & Wear   Telephone: 0191 5210235

Sheffield Industrial Museums Trust
www.simt.co.uk   Telephone: 0114 2367731

Skidby Windmill, Hull, Yorkshire: Uses rollers   Telephone: 01482 884971

Thwaite Putty Mills, Leeds, Yorkshire   Telephone: 0113 2496453

Woodhorn Colliery Museum, Blyth, Northumberland   Telephone: 01670 856968

Woollen Mill, Otterburn, Northumberland   Telephone: 01830 520225

World of Glass, The, Chaldon Way East, St Helens, Lancashire
www.worldofglass.com   Telephone: 08707 444777

Worsbrough Mill Museum, Yorkshire   Telephone: 01226 774527

Wortley Top Forge, Wortley, Nr Stockbridge, Yorkshire
www.topforge.co.uk   Telephone: 0114 2817991

Wales
Bersham Heritage Centre, Nr Wrexham, Denbighshire
www.wrexham.gov.uk/heritage   Telephone: 01978 261529

Big Pit National Mining Museum, Abergavenny, South Wales
www.nmgw.ac.uk   Telephone: 01495 790311

Blaenavon Ironworks, Nr Abergavenny, Monmouthshire
Telephone: 01495 792615

Carew Tidal Watermill, Pembroke   Telephone: 01646 651782

Dyfi Foundry, Nr Machynlleth, Powys: Very rare remains of a charcoal blast
furnace; open access

Felin Isaf, Glan Conwy, Conwy: Watermill   Telephone: 01492 580646

Museum of Welsh Woollen Industry, Newcastle Emlyn, Carmarthen
www.nmgw.ac.uk   Telephone: 01559 370929

Rhondda Heritage Park, Pontypridd, South Wales
www.rhonddaheritagepark.com   Telephone: 01443 682036

Trefriw Woollen Mill, Betws-y-coed, Conwy
www.trefriw-woollen-mills.co.uk   Telephone: 01492 640462

Y Felin, St Dogmaels, Nr Cardigan, Carmarthen: Watermill
Telephone: 01239 613999

Statistics

Just how big some of the changes were that took place in the Industrial Revolution can be seen in the graphs below.

POPULATION

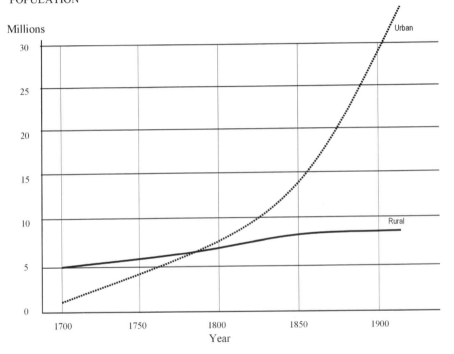

Note the rural population: it is common practice to show this data as a *proportion* of the total population, which gives a falling line for the rural numbers which, in turn, gives an impression of people leaving the rural areas and farming. This is simply not true!

Cities like Halifax, Bolton, Sheffield, Manchester and Liverpool increased their population by around ten times between 1800 and 1900 (the total population of England and Wales rose around 3½ times in the same period). Bradford increased just over twenty-fold!

Breakdown by occupation from the 1851 census:

Agriculture	1,790,000	Wool	280,000
Domestic Service	1,040,000	Shoemaker	270,000
Cotton	530,000	Coal miner	220,000
Building	440,000	Tailor	150,000
Labourer	380,000	Iron	140,000
Milliner/Dressmaker	340,000		

This graph gives an idea of the dramatic increases in some of the basic materials produced during the Industrial Revolution:

MATERIALS

Million Tons of Coal
Thousand Tons of Cotton

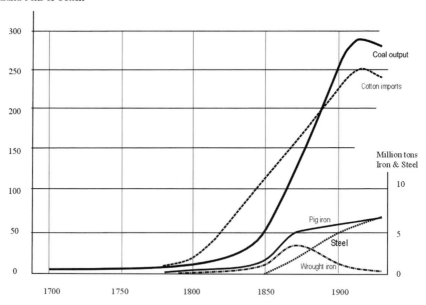

The cotton industry accounted for 2.3% of the total value of exports in 1790, yet by 1830, just 40 years later, it represented 55%.

Notable Inventions and Events

1589   Revd William Lee's frame for knitting stockings.
1622   William Oughtred invents the slide rule.
1698   Thomas Savery patents his steam pump.
1705   Thomas Newcomen creates his first engine.
1706   Henry Mill invents the carriage spring.
1709   Darby smelts iron with coke.
1731   John Hadley produces the first navigational sextant.
1733   John Kay develops the flying shuttle.
1740   Benjamin Huntsman produces crucible steel.
1748   Lewis Paul makes the first wool carding machine.
1755   Thomas Mudge devises the lever escapement for watches.
1764   James Hargreaves designs the spinning jenny.
1768   *The Royal Academy of Arts established by Joshua Reynolds.*
1768   *'Encyclopaedia Britannica' first published.*
1769   James Watt patents his first improvements to the Newcomen engine.
1769   Richard Arkwright makes his water frame.
1770   *Captain James Cook discovers the east coast of Australia.*
1776   *America declares its independence.*
1778   Jesse Ramsden designs a precision screw cutting lathe.
1778   Joseph Bramah launches the valve water closet.
1779   The bridge at Ironbridge erected.
1779   Samuel Crompton develops the spinning mule.
1785   Edmund Cartwright makes the first powered loom.
1787   John Wilkinson makes the first iron boat.
1787   Andrew Meikle makes the first threshing machine.
1789   James Watt patents the double acting engine.
1792   William Murdock demonstrates coal gas lighting.
1793   *The French National Assembly introduces the metric system of measurements.*
1796   *Edward Jenner pioneers vaccination for smallpox.*
1799   *Napoleon proclaims himself First Consul of France.*
1801   Richard Trevithick's first steam road vehicle.
1801   *First Ordnance Survey maps published.*
1804   Trevithick's first steam railway engine.
1805   *Battle of Trafalgar.*
1809   John Heathcoat's lace making machine.
1818   *Mary Shelley writes 'Frankenstein'.*
1823   *Brighton Pier opened – the first pleasure pier in Britain.*
1823   *Charles Babbage invents a calculating machine.*
1825   Joseph Aspdin patents Portland cement.

1831   Michael Faraday generates electricity.
1833   Slavery abolished in the British Empire.
1834   Cyrus McCormack patents a mechanical reaping machine – in America.
1837   Victoria becomes Queen of England.
1838   The first ship to cross the Atlantic under continuous steam – the *Sirius*.
1839   James Nasmyth invents the steam hammer.
1841   Joseph Whitworth standardises threads for screws and bolts.
1843   Brunel's *Great Britain* – the first screw propelled iron merchant ship.
1845   Robert Thompson patents the pneumatic tyre.
1845   Doulton produces glazed stoneware drainpipes.
1851   Joseph Paxton's Crystal Palace built.
1853   Levi Strauss popularises 'jean trowsers' among the California gold miners.
1854   Reinforced concrete invented by W.B. Wilkinson.
1856   W.H. Perkins makes the first useful synthetic dyestuff.
1856   Henry Bessemer develops his converter to mass produce steel.
1865   First transatlantic telephone cable laid linking Britain and America.
1868   Robert Mushet produces tungsten steel.
1877   Bell and Cameron patent refrigeration plant for ships.
1883   Sir Joseph Swan makes rayon.
1884   Charles Parsons' first steam turbine.
1886   Coca Cola is launched in Georgia, USA.

A typical flour mill with a very mixed history. Waterwheel-driven, originally grinding flour then used for a time by Matthew Boulton for metalwork, it later returned to flour grinding, and later still it was aided by a steam engine when the stream flow was low. This is Sarehole Mill, a charming surprise in the suburbs of Birmingham and part of the Tolkien Trail.

Glossary

ATMOSPHERIC ENGINE	An engine that uses the natural air pressure to provide the driving force.
BESSEMER	The inventor of the process to mass produce steel.
BLAST FURNACE	A furnace where the temperature is raised by a blast of air.
BLISTER STEEL	Early form of steel
BLOOMERY	Early furnace for making iron.
BORE	The cutting of a hole in a solid mass.
BREASTSHOT WHEEL	One where the water hits the wheel roughly halfway up.
BURE STONE	A very hard form of quartz used to make grindstones.
CARDING	The process of cleaning and combing raw wool or cotton.
CEMENTATION	Furnace used to make blister steel.
CENTRIFUGAL	The force due to rotation, used in governors to control speed.
CHINTZ	A brilliantly printed cotton material, originally from India.
COKE	Coal that has had the sulphur and water removed by heating.
CONDENSING	The process of changing a gas back to the liquid form, usually by cooling.
CRUCIBLE	A ceramic bowl or container used for heating.
CUPOLA	A form of blast furnace used to re-melt iron.
DISTAFF	A stick used to hold wool in hand weaving.
DOBBY	Mechanism for selecting warp threads to make patterns in woven cloth. Usually mounted high above the loom.
DROP FORGE	A forge that uses drop hammers.
DROP HAMMER	A weight which slides in a frame, usually lifted by steam power and dropped onto the metal being shaped.
FANTAIL	A second, smaller windwheel used to steer the main sails into the wind.
FINERY	A coke-fired hearth used to convert pig iron to wrought iron.
FLUX	A chemical added to a melting process to provide better flow.
FLYING SHUTTLE	A device to carry the weft thread across the loom.
FLYWHEEL	A wheel with the weight concentrated at the outer edge, used to smooth out rotating motion.
FOUNDRY	A workshop where metal is melted.
FULLER'S EARTH	A natural substance which aids the filling out of woollen cloth. Also used in makeup.
FULLING	The process of filling out woollen cloth by washing and beating.
FUSTIAN	A cloth made from a mixture of flax and cotton.
GIN	Device to provide a mechanical drive from a working animal, usually a horse or donkey.
HEALD	A wire with a small ring in the centre used to hold the warp threads in weaving.
JACQUARD	A French inventor who perfected the use of punched cards to determine patterns in woven cloth.

JIG	A device to hold a work piece that guides tools so that each piece is worked in the same way.
LAUNDER	An elevated water channel used to feed waterwheels.
LEAT	A ground level water channel used to take water to a wheel.
LEETE	Old spelling of leat.
LINEN	Cloth woven from flax fibres.
LOOM	A machine for weaving cloth.
MILLSTONE GRIT	A hard stone found in Derbyshire and Yorkshire, used for grindstones and millstones.
MULE	A machine used to mass-produce thread.
NORSE	A very early form of water-driven wheel.
OVERSHOT WHEEL	A type of waterwheel fed at the top.
PIG IRON	A basic form of iron produced by blast furnaces.
PIT WHEEL	The first gear wheel turned by a waterwheel.
PITCHBACK WHEEL	A type of waterwheel fed at the top but in the reverse direction.
POLYMER	A molecular chemical used to make thread; may be natural or synthetic.
PUDDLING	Method used to convert pig iron to wrought iron using oxygen.
REVERBERATORY	A type of furnace where the object being heated is not in direct contact with the fuel.
ROLLER MILL	Flour mill which uses rollers to produce the flour rather than rotating stones.
ROLLING MILL	A factory where heated metal is passed through rollers to change its shape.
ROVING	The thick rope-like result of carding wool or cotton.
SHELLAC	A varnish made from the shellac beetle.
SLITTING MILL	An early form of rolling mill where just the width of the heated metal is formed.
SLIVER	A reduced form of a roving, usually involving further carding.
SMOCK	An old fashioned coat, used to describe windmills of a similar shape.
SPINDLE	A rotating rod used to take up thread.
SPRING STEEL	A group of steels which exhibit the ability to bend and to recover fully.
STOCK	The main beams that carry the sails in a windmill.
SYNTHETIC	Not naturally occurring; made by a chemical process.
TEASEL	The ripened and dried seedpod of the teasel plant.
TENTER BOARD	A frame across which woollen cloth was stretched to dry after fulling and washing.
TENTERHOOKS	The hooks around the edges of a tenter board.
TILT HAMMER	A form of drop hammer where the hammer is lifted by a rotating cam, often waterwheel driven.
TORQUE	The measure of rotational force carried in a shaft or axle.
TURBINE	A propeller-like fan over which gas or liquids are forced, causing it to rotate.
TUYERE	A specially shaped nozzle that allows air to be blown into a furnace.

UNDERSHOT WHEEL	A waterwheel where the water simply passes under the wheel.
VALVE	A device to control the flow of gas or liquids in a pipe.
VITRUVIUS	Roman engineer who first documented waterwheels.
WALLOWER	Name given to the large gear wheel that engages with the pit wheel in a water-driven flour mill.
WARP	The threads that run the length of a piece of material.
WATER FRAME	A machine for thinning and spinning slivers of wool or cotton, originally powered by a waterwheel.
WEFT	The threads that run across the width of a piece of material, crossing the warp threads.
WORSTED	A type of thread made from the best and longest wool fibres, and gives its name to the cloth woven from these threads.
WROUGHT IRON	A pure, malleable form of iron that can be easily shaped and welded.

ALSO IN THIS SERIES

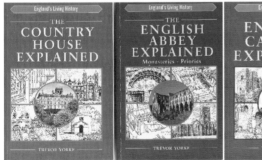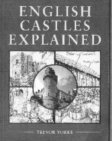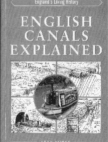

INDEX